GEORGE WASHINGTON
MAN AND MONUMENT

By
MARCUS CUNLIFFE

Introduction by Gordon S. Wood

Published by The Mount Vernon Ladies' Association
through the generosity of

DYKEMA GOSSETT PLLC

MARCUS CUNLIFFE
1922-1990

Marcus Falkner Cunliffe, English by birth and education, taught American history and literature at such prestigious institutions as the Universities of Manchester and Sussex, Harvard University, and the University of California, Berkley. His position as University Professor of George Washington University between 1980 and 1990 brought him in further contact with the subject of this book, one of the most admired biographies of George Washington ever written.

GORDON S. WOOD

Professor Gordon S. Wood is the author of *Radicalism of the American Revolution*, a Pulitzer Prize winner, and of *The Rising Glory of America*. He currently serves as Professor of History at Brown University.

The Mount Vernon Ladies' Association
Mount Vernon, Virginia

ISBN 0-931917-30-1

Printed in the United States of America

Cover Photograph of Houdon's Bust of George Washington by Edward Owen

GEORGE WASHINGTON

MAN AND MONUMENT

TABLE OF CONTENTS

INTRODUCTION

Marcus Cunliffe's *George Washington: Man and Monument,* first published in 1958, was the model of what has now become a veritable genre of history writing — relatively short interpretative essays on Washington's life and image. Over the past 40 years there have been many brief critical studies of Washington as man and as myth. But Cunliffe's little book was the first of its kind, and in nearly all respects it is still the best.

As an Englishman, Cunliffe was an unlikely person to write about the man who led the war for American independence from the British empire. Yet he was not an ordinary Englishman. Although born in England in 1922 and educated at Oriel College, Oxford, Cunliffe from the beginning had an interest in things American. He remembered listening to President Franklin Roosevelt on the radio and watching Jean Harlow and Joan Crawford in American movies. He also learned about America from reading authors such as James Thurber, Stephen Crane,

Ezra Pound and Marianne Moore. Indeed, his first book on America was a study of *The Literature of the United States,* first published in 1954. It has gone through many editions and has sold tens of thousands of copies. What really immersed Cunliffe in things American, however, was a Commonwealth Fund Fellowship that enabled him to spend two years, 1947-49, at Yale University. That experience gave him a new perspective on himself and his homeland. He discovered the charming power his English accent had on Americans, and in the relatively open society of America he became aware of the contrasting constraints of English society. Above all, the experience sparked his scholarly interest in American society and culture. When he returned to England he became one of the founders of American Studies in Great Britain. From 1949 to 1964 he taught American history at the University of Manchester, and then from 1964 to 1980 he was professor of American Studies at the new University of Sussex. During this period he was widely regarded as the foremost scholar of American history in Great Britain.

Much of that reputation came from this little book on Washington. But not at first. Indeed, the American scholarly community initially ignored his 1958 study of Washington. Most of the leading national and state historical journals in the United States did not even bother to review the book. The editors must have thought that the book seemed too essay-like, too lacking in the footnotes and the apparatus of a scholarly study, and too readable to be an important work of history. One of the few scholarly journals that did deign to review the book dismissed it for having too much interpretation and not enough narrative. But that critical interpretative quality is what gave the book its *panache* — the sense of the author's urbane and witty presence on nearly every page — and made the book a pleasure to read. And ultimately that quality is what gave this little gem of a book its staying power. Not only is it still a pleasure to read, but its personal and essay-like character has also become much more acceptable to the professional community. Indeed, the Organization of American Historians recently named Cunliffe's book one of the "ten great books" on Washington ever written.

Unlike many other biographies of Washington, Cunliffe's version is short, with only five chapters. The three middle chapters are brisk accounts of the important phases of Washington's life — his emergence as a prominent Virginia planter, his leadership as commander in chief of the Revolutionary Army, and his presidency. Brief as they are, these chapters nevertheless present us with a remarkably full picture of Washington's life. Cunliffe is a master of the art of condensing complicated material. He leaves out no important events, yet he manages to bring his deft interpretative skills to almost every page. His judgment is nearly always sound, and he has a nice sense of what is significant and what is not.

In his opening and closing chapters of the book — "The Washington Monument" and "The Whole Man" — Cunliffe most clearly reveals his acute historical sense and a central theme of his work — that Washington himself contributed to his becoming a monument. Cunliffe explains better than most biographers, certainly most of those who wrote before his book appeared, that Washington came from another world, from another time and place. Once we grasp this point, Cunliffe suggests, we can more easily understand the peculiar monumental character of the man. Washington, writes Cunliffe, lived in "a reticent era." Acutely aware that people did not value the open expression of emotions, Washington more than most of his contemporaries practiced restraint and self-control. His aloofness was notorious and he worked at it. He actually tried to create a distant and severe public persona. Despite his outward modesty, Washington had no doubt that he was an extraordinary man and he was not ashamed of it. He lived in an era where distinctions of rank were still acceptable and "elitism" was not an opprobrious term. He took for granted the differences between himself and more ordinary men. And when he could not take these differences for granted, he cultivated them. Since he lived in such a different world from our own, our modern efforts to humanize him, to make him more like us, Cunliffe suggests, "run the risk of falsifying — of losing the essential truth of his personality."

But it was not only an age of reticence that Washington lived in, it was a classical age, an age that "differed profoundly from ours." Washington, says Cunliffe, is "better understood within a classical framework than as a man of modern times." Roman duty, Roman *gravitas,* Roman virtue — these were the republican terms that the Revolutionaries invoked, and Cunliffe was one of the first historians to appreciate their significance. More than most of his Revolutionary colleagues, Washington tried to act the part of a Roman patriot. He loved Joseph Addison's play *Cato;* he saw it over and over and even incorporated its lines into his correspondence. Many of his actions were governed by classical models, including the greatest act of his life — his resignation as commander in chief of the American forces. The surrendering of his sword to Congress in December 1783, his dramatic retirement from power, was unprecedented in modern times. Victorious generals did not relinquish their arms and simply return to their farms. Cromwell, William of Orange, Marlborough — all had sought political rewards commensurate with their military achievements. But not Washington. All he wanted, as he had promised his countrymen in 1775, was for the soldiers "to return to our Private Stations in the bosom of a free, peaceful, & happy Country." In his effort to live up to the age's image of a classical disinterested patriot, Washington was well aware of the effect his resignation would have on the world. He knew at once that he had established his reputation as a modern Cincinnatus.

It may bore us, says Cunliffe, to learn again and again that Washington was a second Cincinnatus, "yet there is still vitality in the cliché." Washington "looked and behaved like a classical hero," possessing all the qualities that were needed to lead an army or a government. But, according to Cunliffe, he was more than a classical leader. Washington became the symbol of America; he proved in his own person the soundness of the country. Indeed, he became "so merged with America that his is one of the names on the land, the presences in the air.... The man is the monument; the monument *is* America."

Cunliffe admired America just as he admired Washington, but not uncritically. Perhaps because he viewed America through Washington's eyes, he came to worry about what he took to be the lack of integrity and dignity in many of the nation's leaders. Despite his concern with what was happening in modern America, he accepted an invitation to move across the Atlantic and take up a university professorship at George Washington University in 1980. He believed that a university in the nation's capital was the best place in the world to practice American Studies. His untimely death in 1990 — he was only 68 — deprived us of one of America's most important and insightful historical interpreters. Fortunately, however, he left us this brilliant and delightful book on Washington.

Gordon S. Wood
August 1998

CHAPTER ONE

THE WASHINGTON MONUMENT

The shades of Vernon to remotest time, will be trod with awe; the banks of Potomac will be hallowed ground.

Charles Pinckney Sumner,
Eulogy on the Illustrious George Washington, February 1800

Does not that Colossal Unit remind all who gaze at it... that there is one name in American history above all other names, one character more exalted than all other characters... one bright particular star in... our firmament, whose guiding light and peerless lustre are for all men and all ages...?

Robert C. Winthrop,
*Dedication of the Washington
National Monument*, February 1885

The Washington Monument in Washington, D.C., is, we are told, 555 feet high – higher than the spires of Cologne Cathedral, higher than St. Peter's in Rome, much higher than the Pyramids. When George Washington died, in December 1799, the new federal capital had already been named in his honor. As a further gesture, the House of Representatives resolved that a marble monument should be built, "so designed as to commemorate the great events of his military and political life." Washington's body was to be entombed beneath the shrine. But for various reasons, some unedifying, it was never erected. The soaring obelisk that we call the Washington Monument was a later project, not completed until a hundred years after George Washington had achieved victory and independence for his nation. Many thousand tons of concrete are buried under its base. Yet the bones of the man it celebrates are not there either; they repose a few miles away, in the vault of his Mount Vernon home.

Innumerable tourists visit Mount Vernon. It is a handsome place, as they can testify, refurbished with taste and maintained in immaculate order. But the ghosts have been all too successfully exorcised in the process; Mount Vernon is less a house than a kind of museum-temple. We know that George Washington lived and died there; we do not *feel* the fact, any more than we can recapture the presence of William Shakespeare at Stratford-on-Avon. Both men are baffling figures to us, prodigious and indistinct. One American writer has said of them that "England's greatest contribution to the world is the works of Shakespeare; America's is the character of Washington." On this sort of scale are they measured; and it is not a human scale.

There is a difference, of course. Whereas we can find out almost nothing about Shakespeare, we have a vast amount of information about Washington. Only one blank portrait of Shakespeare exists; the portraits of Washington – some of them apparently excellent likenesses – require three volumes to list in full. There are no autobiographical fragments from Shakespeare's hand; Washington's letters and diaries fill over forty volumes, in printed form. Hardly any of his contemporaries mentioned Shakespeare; scores of friends, acquaintances and casual callers set down for us their impressions of George Washington. A strange obscurity envelops the figure of Shakespeare; Washington stood in the glaring limelight of world fame. But the result – optically, so to speak – is similar: the darkness and the dazzle both have an effect of concealment.

Trying in vain to discern the actual man behind the huge, impersonal, ever-growing legend, biographers have reacted in various ways. In the case of Shakespeare, some have denied his authorship of the plays and have attempted to substitute a more plausible bard; a Bacon or even a Marlowe. The reaction in the case of Washington has naturally been otherwise. No one, in the face of such a quantity of evidence, can pretend that he never existed, or that some other man deserves the credit. But he has become entombed in his own myth – a metaphorical Washington Monument that hides from us the lineaments of the real man. Year by year this monument has grown, like a cairn to which each passer-by adds a stone. Pamphlet, speech, article and book; pebble, rubble, stone and boulder have piled up. As far back as 1885, Robert C. Winthrop of Massachusetts, speaking at the dedication of the Monument, ruefully asked: "What can any man say of Washington, which has not already been rendered as familiar as household words...? How could I hope to glean anything from a field long ago so carefully... reaped by such [biographers] as John Marshall and Jared Sparks, by Guizot and Edward Everett and Washington Irving...?" Anecdote, monograph, panegyric: whatever the level and value of each contribution it has – ironically, in the instance of more important contributions – tended to smother what it seeks to disclose.

Worse, Washington has become not merely a mythical figure, but a myth of suffocating dullness, the victim of civic elephantiasis. There is a drouth, a dearth of emotion, a heaviness well caught in John Updike's poem "February 22":

More than great successes, we love great failures.
Lincoln is Messiah; he, merely Caesar.
He suffered greatness like a curse.
He fathered our country, we feel, without great joy.

Confronted by the shelves and shelves of "Washingtoniana" – all those sonorous, repetitious, reverential items, the set pieces in adulation that are impossible to read without yawning – we seek some sour antidote to so much saccharine, and tend to agree with Emerson: "Every hero becomes a bore at last.... They cry up the virtues of George Washington – 'Damn George Washington!' is the poor Jacobin's whole speech and confutation." When we have allowed ourselves the relief of this irreverence, though, the monument still looms before us, and must be reckoned with before we can get to grips with Washington the man. We may suspect, however, that myth and man can never be entirely separated, and that valuable clues to Washington's temperament, as well as his public stature, lie in this fact.

The first thing to note, in exploring the monument, is that the myth-making process was at work during Washington's own lifetime. *"Vae, puto deus fio,"* the dying Roman emperor Vespasian is supposed to have murmured: "Alas, I think I am about to become a god." Such a mixture of levity and magnificence would have been foreign to George Washington. Yet he might with justice have thought the same thing as he lay on his deathbed at Mount Vernon in 1799. Babies were being christened after him as early as 1775, and while he was still President, his countrymen paid to see him in waxwork effigy. To his admirers he was "godlike Washington," and his detractors complained to one another that he was looked upon as a "demi-god" whom it was treasonable to criticize. "O Washington!" declared Ezra Stiles of Yale (in a sermon of 1783). "How I do love thy name! How have I often adored and blessed thy God, for creating and forming thee the great ornament of human kind!... our very enemies stop the madness of their fire in full volley, stop the illiberality of their slander at thy name, as if rebuked from Heaven with a – 'Touch not mine Anointed, and do my Hero no harm!' Thy fame is of sweeter perfume than Arabian spices. Listening angels shall catch the odor, waft it to heaven, and perfume the universe!"

Here indeed is a legend in the making. His contemporaries vied in their tributes – all intended to express the idea that there was something superhuman about George Washington. We need not labor the point that, after death, "godlike Washington" passed still further into legend, his surname appropriated for one American state, seven mountains, eight streams, ten lakes, thirty-three counties; for nine American colleges; for one hundred and twenty-one American towns and villages. His birthday has long been a national holiday. His visage is on coins and banknotes and postage stamps; his portrait (usually the snaffle-mouthed, immensely grave "Athenaeum" version by Gilbert Stuart) is hung in countless corridors and offices. His head – sixty feet from chin to scalp – has been carved out of a mountainside in South Dakota. There are statues of him all over the United States – and all over the world: you can see them in London and in Paris, in Buenos Aires and Rio de Janeiro, in Caracas and Budapest and Tokyo.

All these are outward signs of Washington's heroic standing in the world. But we should look a little more closely at the monument. If the metaphor may be extended, we can observe that the monument has four sides: four roles that Washington has been made to play for posterity's sake. The four are not sharply distinct – nothing is, in this misty Valhalla – but it is worth our while to take a glance at each of them before turning to the actual events from which the legends emanated. This is, of course, not to argue that Washington is undeserving of praise;

his merits were genuine and manifold. The crucial point is that the real merits were enlarged and distorted into unreal attitudes, and that this overblown Washington is the one who occurs immediately to us when his name is mentioned. He might occur in any or all of the following four guises: a) *the Copybook Hero;* b) *the Father of His People;* c) *the Disinterested Patriot;* d) *the Revolutionary Leader.* These are all guises of the hero figure. In each, Washington is a member of a pantheon; and for each pantheon there is a kind of antipantheon of heroes who fell from grace.

THE COPYBOOK HERO

Washington's life lay completely within the eighteenth century, though only just. But Washington as he has descended to us is largely a creation of the nineteenth-century English-speaking world, with its bustling, didactic, evangelical emphasis. This is the world of tracts and primers, of Chambers's *Miscellanies* and McGuffey's *Readers,* of Samuel Smiles and Horatio Alger, of mechanics' institutes and lyceum lectures, of autograph albums and gift annuals. It is the age of Masonic rituals. Freemasons were prominent in the ceremony both for the start of the Washington Monument in 1848, and at its dedication in 1885. Bazaars and bridges are opened, foundation stones laid, prizes and certificates distributed, drunkards admonished and rescued, slaves emancipated. It is, in the convenient term of David Riesman, the age of the "inner-directed" personality whose essential attributes are summed up in the titles of Smiles's various works – *Self-Help, Thrift, Duty, Character* – or in a short poem of Emerson's that is also called "Character."

> *The stars set, but set not his hope:*
> *Stars rose; his faith was earlier up:*
> *Fixed on the enormous galaxy*
> *Deeper and older seemed his eye;*
> *And matched his sufferance sublime*
> *The taciturnity of time...*

Character is the key word in the copybook view of George Washington, as we have already seen in the statement linking him with Shakespeare.[1] Lord Brougham is of the same opinion: "The test of the

---

[1] It is emphasized in 1843 by Daniel Webster, in an oration at Bunker Hill. America, he says, owes a considerable debt to the Old World. She has repaid it in large part by furnishing "to the world the character of Washington! And if our American institutions had done nothing else, that alone would have entitled them to the respect of mankind.:"

progress of mankind will be their appreciation of the character of Washington."

The enterprising Mason Locke Weems, a Victorian before the Victorian era, was the first to fit Washington into what was to become the pattern of the century. His aim in writing a pamphlet biography of Washington was, Weems explained to a publisher in 1800, to bring out "his Great Virtues. 1 His Veneration for the Diety [*sic*], or Religious Principles. 2 His patriotism. 3d. His magnanimity [*sic*]. 4 his Industry. 5 his Temperance and Sobriety. 6. His Justice, &c &c." Here is the copybook canon. Weems was not quite as high-minded as this statement might suggest, though there is no reason to doubt that he shared the general American veneration for Washington. As he told the same publisher, his proposal could win them "pence and popularity." At any rate, he did not hesitate to fabricate incidents, or to style himself "Rector" of the non-existent parish of Mount Vernon. His pamphlet grew into a book, embodying stage by stage the famous false Weemsian anecdotes: Washington chopping down the cherry tree ("*I can't tell a lie, Pa; you know I can't tell a lie. I did cut it with my hatchet." – Run to my arms you dearest boy, cried his father in transports*); Washington upbraiding his schoolmates for fighting – an episode that gradually disappeared from the record, since later generations found it priggish ("*You shall never, boys, have my consent to a practice so shocking! shocking even in slaves and dogs; then how utterly scandalous in little boys at school, who ought to look on one another as brothers*"); young Washington throwing a stone across the Rappahannock (*It would be no easy matter to find a man, now-a-days, who could do it*); Washington's providential escape at Braddock's defeat (*A famous Indian warrior, who acted a leading part in that bloody tragedy, was often heard to swear, that "Washington was not born to be killed by a bullet! For . . . I had seventeen fair fires at him with my rifle, and after all could not bring him to the ground!"*); Washington discovered – by a Quaker "of the respectable family and name of Potts, if I mistake not" – praying at Valley Forge (*As he approached the spot . . . whom should he behold . . . but the commander in chief of the American armies on his knees at prayer!*); and so on.

All through the book Weems strove to show how inseparably "duty and advantage" went together. Thus, kindness to his elder brother brought George the Mount Vernon estate when his brother died childless save for one ailing infant; and exemplary conduct subsequently won him the hand of the widow Custis, whose "*wealth* was equal, at least, to one hundred thousand dollars!" The homily was irresistible; by 1825 Weems's biography had gone through forty editions, and forty more were to appear in due course. The cherry-tree story – eventually incorporated in McGuffey's highly popular *Readers* – became a special favorite in copybook lore. Invention was added to invention in Morrison Heady's juvenile life of Washington, *The Farmer Boy, and How He Became Commander-in-Chief* (1863). Heady describes how Jerry, a little slave boy, was wrongly blamed for cutting down the tree, and how young George saved him from a flogging by confessing to the crime. (Ever after, according to Heady, Jerry "loved his noble little master to distraction.") Indeed, in the secular hagiology of the period – the equivalent of Saint Lawrence with his gridiron or Saint Catherine with her wheel – Washington and the tree joined the company of Newton and William Tell with their respective apples, Watt with his kettle, Bruce with his spider, Columbus with his egg, King Alfred with his cakes, Sir Philip Sidney with his water bottle.

But Washington's whole career was pressed into service, not merely one episode. The expense accounts that he kept during the Revolutionary War were printed in facsimile, as proof of his patriotic frugality and business efficiency. His religious opinions were recast, by Weems and others, into the nineteenth-century mold. One tale has it that he left the Anglican Church for Presbyterianism. According to another fable, he secretly joined the Baptists. It is unnecessary to emphasize that such notions, whether they originated in the fertile mind of Weems or elsewhere, were usually untrue in detail and unhistorical in a larger way. Weems and his successors were not concerned with what they would have thought of as scholastic pedantry. Their object, quite deliberately, was to point a moral and adorn a tale. They agreed with the words of Henry Lee, in praise of Weems (and quoted on Weems's title page): "No biographer deserves more applause than he whose chief purpose is to entice the young mind to the affectionate love of virtue, by personifying it in the character most dear to these states." Or, as Horatio Hastings Weld said in his *Pictorial Life of George Washington* (1845): "The first word of infancy should be mother, the second father, the third WASHINGTON." The boy hero of Frances Hodgkin Burnett's *Little Lord Fauntleroy* (1886), a model child, says: "My papa was a soldier, and he was a very brave man – as brave as George Washington . . . . Once I used to be rather afraid of things – in the dark, you know; but when I thought about the soldiers in the Revolution and George Washington – it cured me."

We may feel that Weems and the rest of the copy book moralizers must share some of the blame for blurring our image of Washington. In their defense, we should recognize that they did not mean to turn

Washington into a plaster saint. They were well aware of this tendency. "In most of the elegant orations pronounced to his praise," wrote Weems, "you see nothing of Washington below *the clouds* . . . 'tis only Washington the HERO, and the Demi-god . . . Washington the *sun beam* in council, or the *storm* in war." Weems wanted to humanize him, as well as present him as a copybook character. So did the propagators of another once-popular legend, not to be found in Weems, that the youthful Washington had tamed a colt too energetically and perhaps caused its death. One aim of this anecdote was to portray Washington as a high-mettled adolescent – though also admittedly a moral young man, since he readily confessed his part in the accidental death of the young animal. Certainly there is not much of the marmoreal in Weems's racy narrative; with its aid, he managed to impose his apocryphal Washington on a whole nation for a whole century. Weems would no doubt claim that he could not have done so if people had not wished to believe that this was the truth. Washington's family motto was *Exitus acta probat;* to suit himself and vindicate his fictions, Weems might mistranslate this as "The end justifies the means." At any rate, what he depicted was Washington as the man without faults, and with all the nineteenth-century virtues, from courage to punctuality, from modesty to thrift – and all within human compass, and all crowned by success.

THE FATHER OF HIS PEOPLE

Nevertheless, Washington did inhabit the clouds in the estimation of a great many people. In the well-worn phrase of Henry Lee (also used by John Marshall), he was *first in war, first in peace, and first in the hearts of his countrymen* – first chronologically and emotionally: America's first commander in chief and first President. He was the prime native hero, a necessary creation for a new country. It was only natural to replace "George Guelf" (Jefferson's description) by George Washington. Thus Rip Van Winkle, after a twenty-year sleep, returns to his native village to find, among other things, that its old Dutch inn is now the Union Hotel. On the inn sign "he recognized . . . the ruby face of King George, under which he had smoked so many a peaceful pipe; but even this was singularly metamorphosed. The red coat was changed for one of blue and buff, a sword was held in the hand instead of a sceptre, the head was decorated in a cocked hat, and underneath was painted in large characters, GENERAL WASHINGTON." This was in fiction; the substitution was made actual in New York, where the base of a destroyed statue of George III was used to display one of Washington.[2] Hence, too, the observation made by the European traveler Paul Svinin, as early as 1815: "Every American considers it his sacred duty to have a likeness of Washington in his home, just as we have images of God's saints." For America, Washington was the originator and vindicator, both patron saint *and* defender of the faith, in a curiously timeless fashion, as if he were Charlemagne, Saint Joan and Napoleon Bonaparte telescoped into one person.

After him, only Abraham Lincoln has rivaled his national glory. In some respects Lincoln is now a more relevant hero than Washington: his Second Inaugural is the New Testament among national documents to the Old Testament of Washington's Farewell Address. In the words of William G. Rutherford's *Abraham Lincoln: Plough-Boy, Statesman, Patriot,* a late-nineteenth-century book for children: "The names of three men – Christopher Columbus, George Washington, and Abraham Lincoln – stand apart in the history of America. . . . The American people honour the man who first dared to cross the waste of waters. . . . They are proud of their first President. . . . But when they speak of 'The Saviour of the Nation' and the liberator of the slave, their hearts glow. . . ." Yet Lincoln is still human, time-bound and even time-stained. One cannot quite imagine him in a painting like Brumidi's *Apotheosis of Washington,* which is on the dome of the National Capitol and shows Washington flanked by Freedom and Victory. Nor can one imagine American critics objecting to a fictional account of Lincoln (or for that matter any other American hero, with the possible exception of Robert E. Lee) as they object, for example, to Thackeray's treatment of Washington in *The Virginians.* "Why," one angry reviewer wrote, "this is the very essence of falsehood. Washington was not like other men; and to bring his lofty character down to the level of the vulgar passions of common life, is to give the lie to the grandest chapter in the uninspired annals of the human race." As another critic admonished Thackeray: "Washington's character has come to us spotless, and if you impute to him the little follies that have belonged to other great men, the majestic apparition you have called up may visit you, pure and white as you see him in Houdon's statue, and freeze you into silence with his calm, reproachful gaze."

This is a remarkable threat, and it conveys the intensity of American feeling for Washington a century ago. A similar protective reverence was

---

[2] And at Nassau Hall, Princeton College, where in 1783 the trustees commissioned from Charles Willson Peale, a portrait of Washington as a substitute for "the picture of the late king [George II] of Great Britain, which was torn away by a ball from the American artillery in the battle of Princeton."

revealed by Jared Sparks of Massachusetts when he edited Washington's correspondence in the 1830s. He was afterwards accused of having tampered with the text in order to present Washington in a more dignified light. By the standards of his day Sparks, a Harvard historian who eventually became president of the college, was a diligent archivist and able historian. But he does seem to have omitted or altered passages that might be regarded as vulgar; to cite two notorious instances, Washington's reference to "Old Put" was changed to "General Putnam," while "but a flea-bite at present" was rendered as "Totally inadequate to our demands at this time." Consciously or unconsciously, Sparks reflected the American belief that "Washington was not like other men." To admit failings in him was therefore to attack the very fabric of America. Hence, likewise, the universal American horror at men like Benedict Arnold, the betrayers of Washington and of their fatherland. In committing treason they were also deemed guilty of sacrilege.

Some of his countrymen – notably John Adams – were a little irked by the Washington cult. They felt that adulation had gone too far – as in the suggestion that God had denied Washington children of his own so that he might assume paternity for the whole nation. Tom Paine was one of several pamphleteers who, during the 1790s, began to attack the national hero as cold and conservative. James Callender, the author of *The Prospect Before Us,* a diatribe against John Adams's administration, rivaled Paine in dubbing Washington a "traitor." But even Adams was prepared to defend Washington as a native product against all challengers from other lands, with the proviso that Washington's virtues were America's virtues, rather than vice versa. Washington was great because his country bred such qualities, and shaped their fulfillment. Here, then, are two conceptions of Washington the Father of His People, as transcendent American and as representative American. But in either case he was (as Rufus Griswold said) "identified with the country" to an unparalleled degree. "He was its mind; it was his image and illustration." Certainly this is true in terms of nomenclature. The name of Washington, as we have seen, spread all over the land; and it was adopted for people as well as places. There was *Washington* Irving; one of Walt Whitman's brothers was called *George Washington* Whitman; and for the ex-slave boy Booker Taliaferro, to adopt the surname of *Washington* was in a way to take on American citizenship. Others, inspired by classroom patriotism, expressed their own desire to be accepted by adding their modest tributes to the praise of Washington. Mary Antin, an immigrant from Russian Poland, fell in love with George Washington as a schoolgirl in Boston. Her autobiography, *The*

Promised Land (1912), describes how, in an ecstasy of Americanism, she composed a poem to her hero and had it printed in a Boston newspaper.

Washington's name and fame were invoked for decades after his death to symbolize national patriotism and unity. His Farewell Address, printed and quoted innumerable times, took on fresh relevance with the heightening of sectional tension between North and South. Edward Everett's famous, much-repeated address, "The Character of Washington," insisted in the 1850s that the preservation of the union was Washington's foremost concern; "and if – which Heaven forbid – the day shall ever arrive when his parting counsels on that head shall be forgotten, on that day, it may as mournfully as truly be said, that Washington has lived in vain." Members of the nativist American or Know-Nothing party of the same era were fond of citing a supposed instruction by General Washington at a crucial moment in the Revolution: "Put none but Americans on guard tonight" – meaning of course native-born Americans. After the Civil War Washington became a symbol of reconciliation between North and South, and of the triumph of Union against seemingly hopeless odds. The "truncated shaft" of his Monument, in Winthrop's words, had stood unfinished for more than twenty years. With the completion of Reconstruction, however, the building of the obelisk could be renewed. The other principal speaker at the 1885 dedication of the Monument, the Honorable John W. Daniel, was a Virginian, able to stress the Old Dominion heritage of Washington, and couple it with Winthrop's Massachusetts as if the Civil War had been a mere minor aberration.

THE DISINTERESTED PATRIOT

As father of his people, Washington naturally stands apart – though perhaps conceding a lesser share to Benjamin Franklin. ("The history of our Revolution," wrote the exasperated John Adams, "will be one continued lie from one end to the other. The essence of the whole will be that Dr. Franklin's electric rod smote the earth and out sprung General Washington. That Franklin electrised him with his rod, and thenceforward these two conducted all the policy negotiations, legislatures, and war.") As Disinterested Patriot, he is one of a select pantheon. Against nearly all historical precedent, he retired to private life twice, after holding the two most powerful offices in America. Marveling at such humility, men could only compare him with Timoleon of Corinth, who brought peace to Sicily and lived out his days there; with Cincinnatus –

Thus, when of old, from his paternal farm
Rome had her rigid Cincinnatus arm,
Th' illustrious peasant rushed to the field;
Soon are the haughty Volsii taught to yield;
His country sav'd the solemn triumph o'er,
He tills his native acres as before.

(these lines by the Maryland poet Charles Henry Wharton, are from "A Poetical Epistle" addressed to Washington in 1779); or with the younger Cato of Addison's play (two of whose lines – "'Tis not in mortals to command success" and "The post of honour is a private station" – Washington was fond of quoting). They could contrast him with the more numerous antipantheon of interested patriots, which included Sulla and Caesar, Wallenstein, Cromwell and – in the eighteenth century – the three figures often called "Great": Peter of Russia, Frederick of Prussia, and Napoleon of France. Of these, while admitting their talents, Edward Everett was scathingly dismissive. The Tsar Peter, for example, "united the wisdom of a philosopher and the policy of a great prince with the tastes of a satyr, the manners of a barbarian and the passions of a fiend; guilty of crimes so hideous and revolting" – Everett assured his American audience – "that if I attempted to describe them, I should drive you shrieking from this hall. You surely would not permit me to place the name of Washington in comparison with his." The contrast between Washington and Napoleon Bonaparte was startlingly evident; and Byron, who spoke of Washington in this connection as "the Cincinnatus of the West," was one of many who dwelt on it. Thus Chateaubriand, the French romantic writer, inserted in his *Voyage en Amérique* an extended comparison between the two men, lamenting that for all his genius Napoleon had lacked the liberty-loving decency of the American. "The republic of Washington subsists; the empire of Bonaparte is no more." Moreover, not all the doings of the few disinterested patriots could bear close scrutiny:

But in all the actions of those other great captains, their glory was always mingled with violence, pain and labor: so as some of them have been touched with reproach, and others with repentance.

The words are Plutarch's, in praise of Timoleon; but he goes on to admit that even Timoleon once behaved viciously. It would seem that we are left, among the pure patriots, with almost no one except the half-legendary Lucius Quinctius Cincinnatus to rival George Washington. The group as a whole is a classical assembly (we could add Epaminondas, Agesilaus, Brutus and a few others), and Washington's place in it contributes still further to the timeless, dreamlike unreality of our vision of him.

His role here fits well into the Classical Revival mood of early nineteenth-century America. (It does, though, conflict a little with the cozier, more domesticated Weemsian view. We should remember that Horatio Greenough's colossal marble statue of Washington in a toga was ridiculed in the 1850s. A tourist who went to look at Greenough's work found that "some irreverent heathen had taken the pains to climb up and insert a large 'plantation' cigar between the lips of the *pater patriae. . . .* I cold not help thinking . . . that if Washington had looked less like the Olympic Jove, and more like himself, not even the vagabond who perpetrated the trick of the cigar would have dared or dreamed of such a desecration.") And, as Robert P. Hay points out, Washington was quite often alluded to in biblical terms, as the "American Moses" who had led his people out of bondage into the promised land.

THE REVOLUTIONARY LEADER

This is an idea of Washington held mainly outside the United States, and especially during the last decade of his life, though it went on reverberating through the next hundred years. The conception has a strong tincture of ideology. It is of Washington as the chieftain, the liberator, the champion of nationalism, and the victor in the first great revolution of modern times. In this role he appears as the unwitting chairman of a vehement, valiant, swashbuckling committee, whose other members are men like Lafayette, Thaddeus Kosciuszko, Toussaint L'Ouverture, Bernardo O'Higgins of Chile, Bolívar and Garibaldi,[3] with vacant places left by Iturbide and others who disgraced themselves. Chinese patriots including Sun Yat-sen and the youthful Mao Tse-tung admired the selfless persistence they associated with Washington. To the French, trying to achieve a revolution of their own on the American model, Washington naturally had a particular significance. "Vasington," "Vashington," or "Wassington," as he was variously known in France, was a symbol, to be evoked in plays like Billardon de Sauvigny's *Vasington ou la Liberté du Nouveau Monde* – a four-act tragedy performed

---

[3] The flagship of the flotilla that supported Garibaldi in his Sicilian campaign of 1860 was named the Washington. Many instances of foreign reactions are mentioned in Richard B. Morris, The Emerging Nations and the American Revolution (New York, 1970).

in Paris in 1791. Half a century later the French author-statesman Lamartine spoke of Washington as "the symbol of modern liberty."

When the Latin-American countries rebelled against Spanish rule, he became for them also a symbol. And for all countries involved in revolutionary war he provided a practical inspiration, of a citizen soldier commanding a citizen army. At the head of his "banditti" (as the English often called them) he is hunted, thwarted, lonely, outnumbered, maintains midwinter vigils. "Without shoes and without bread," confronting well-clad and well-fed professionals, Washington's men are the original ragged-trousered philanthropists – after who, according to one story, the French sans-culottes were named.

The way is hard for Washington. But the Cause, and the reading of Tom Paine, sustains him; he crossed the Delaware, arms folded and head held high, amid the chunks of ice . . . and triumph is eventually his. It is all an intoxicating brew of republicanism, conspiracy, Freemasonry ("Vasington," like Lafayette, Mozart and a number of other liberal-minded Europeans of the period, was a Mason). It is a period of new fashions in dress, new anthems, new banners (in one of the familiar Washington myths, he collaborates with Betsy Ross in devising the American flag). Lafayette sends Washington "the main key of the fortress of despotism" (i.e., of the Bastille, which the Paris mob had stormed in 1789; the key still reposes at Mount Vernon, without inconveniencing anyone, since the Bastille was demolished). "It is," Lafayette writes, "a tribute which I owe as a son to my adopted father, as an aide-de-camp to my general, as *a missionary of liberty to its patriarch*" (my italics). Another missionary of liberty salutes the patriarch in 1792. This is the poet Coleridge, then a Cambridge undergraduate, whose rooms in college have been described as "a veritable left-wing cell of those days"; as a gesture of defiance to the established order, a blow for freedom against reaction, he publicly drinks Washington's health in a taproom. So much had Washington become an ideological symbol. He is a somber, prophetic figure, not a real person, in William Blake's "America":

Washington spoke: "Friends of America! Look over the Atlantic sea;
A bended bow is lifted in heaven, and a heavy iron chain
Descends, link by link, from Albion's cliffs across the sea, to bind
Brothers and sons of America till our faces pale and yellow,
Heads deprest, voices weak, eyes downcast, hands work-bruis'd,
Feet bleeding on the sultry sands, and the furrows of the whip
Descend to generations that in future times forget."

In Latin America, a few years later, Washington the Revolutionary Leader, continues to serve. Bolívar carries a portrait medallion of him. Where he and the United States have led, in breaking loose from European bondage, other American nations can follow. His doctrine no less than his example is a guide; Washington's Farewell Address is read and cited throughout Spanish America, until its injunctions are almost as influential there as in his own country. Statesmen quote him; plazas are named after him. Possibly we may discern the dim outlines of yet another, fifth role for Washington, one that he *might* have played – as presiding genius for the never-found Atlantis known as Pan-America.

In Tsarist Russia, during his lifetime, Washington is praised as an ideal figure. In 1826, a Decembrist republican – in other words, a would-be radical – declares that "the name of Washington, the friend and benefactor of the people, will pass from generation to generation." Michael Bakunin the revolutionary, on a short visit to the United States in 1861, took the trouble to acquire a Washington autograph.

And back in the United States we catch a glimpse of the myth-making process at work through the *Autobiography* of Moncure Daniel Conway, an unorthodox Virginian who strongly disapproved of slavery. Conway recalls writing a story for children at the end of 1859 – a story that sought to combine various popular legends. In Conway's tale, "Excalibur," the magical sword of King Arthur, passes into the hands of Frederick the Great of Prussia. The sword enables him to win his wars. Subsequently, Frederick sends it to Washington, engraved with the words: "From the oldest General in the world to the greatest" – an attractive though untrue legend. Moncure plays with the idea that John Brown, who seized a descendant of Washington as a hostage for his raid on Harper's Ferry, also came into possession of a sword of Washington's that was actually Excalibur. In fact, Brown did acquire a sword inherited by Washington's great-grandnephew, Colonel Lewis Washington, his hostage. This sword was supposed to have been presented by Frederick the Great. And John Brown, fascinated by the weapon, buckled it on and wore it in his improvised fortress at Harper's Ferry.

Washington is, of course, only one among many great men who have been made to serve as object lessons to succeeding generations. Each age seeks its own inspiration or comfort in the past. The dead are merely the dead unless we choose to resurrect them; they live in us and through us. Our interest in them is egocentric: we wish to learn from them what *we* are like.

There is nothing iniquitous in interpreting Washington according to the standards of the moment. That is more or less what historians have always done, whatever their subject, though some have been more scrupulous than others in the handling of evidence, and though it is fatal for them to be too aware of what they are doing. Our age sets greater store than Weems's or Jared Sparks's by historical accuracy. But when will there ever be an "impartial" biography of Adolph Hitler – or even of Franklin Roosevelt or Winston Churchill?

Nor is Washington the only great man to have been enlarged to giant scale. Louis XIV dedicated himself to the construction of his own monument – the elaboration of a hugely inflated myth of a *Roi Soleil*. Marlborough was given a dukedom, and a palace so prodigious that it makes Mount Vernon look like a gardener's cottage.[4] Miss Consuelo Vanderbilt, the American heiress who married one of Marlborough's descendants, tells us that the kitchens of Blenheim Palace are five hundred yards from the dining room (with disastrous results for the food). Nelson's grateful countrymen gave him a viscountcy and, after Trafalgar, a whole square in London, dominated by the Nelson Column. Wellington won a dukedom and a dizzying quantity of other honors (including enough trophies to stock a sizable museum). They lent their names to regiments, schools, public houses, battleships. Napoleon Bonaparte is a still more formidable figure to posterity. The subject of literally thousands of books (three or four times as many as Washington, one would guess), he is perpetuated also in a network of highways, a coinage, a legal system – in short, in the entire fabric of his nation, not to mention other European countries.

Nevertheless, there is probably nothing quite like the Washington Monument in history. There have been various conceptions of him, and they have altered somewhat from generation to generation. But none of the principal conceptions – the sides of the monument – has been wildly at variance with the others, and none has been discredited. Could anyone who weighed his words soberly say this, as Gladstone did of Washington, about any other celebrity of Washington's time or since?

> If, among all the pedestals supplied by history for public
> characters of extraordinary nobility and purity, I saw one higher
> than all the rest, and if I were required, at a moment's notice, to
> name the fittest occupant for it, I think my choice, at any time

---

[4] Edward Everett's "Character of Washington" address rams home the contrast between the frugal, upright Washington with his modest home and the Duke of Marlborough, a great commander but (according to Everett) a megalomaniac miser, "despicable under the shadow of his thick-woven laurels." See vol. 4 of Everett's Orations and Speeches on Various Occasions (Boston, 1885).

during the last forty-five years, would have lighted, and it would now light upon Washington!

No one else has been so thoroughly venerated, and so completely frozen into legend. The name *Napoleon* may evoke a picture of a brilliant general, a ruthless tyrant, a restless exile, or perhaps a faithless husband. But the picture, however grand or highly colored, is credible; it is of a recognizable man. The same is true of the name *Nelson,* which at once conjures up images of a dashing public career and a gaudy private one. It is even true of *Wellington,* the Iron Duke, who at many points bears a close resemblance to George Washington. *Wellington* suggests a hero, a personage, a stern and rather unapproachable being, but still a human being. But what does the name *Washington* convey? It may well mean a place; and if you establish that you mean *George Washington,* it could be the name of an institution; and if you insist that you mean the original owner and helpless bequeather of the name, then you are left with — what? Anecdotes that are mostly fictitious and not very lifelike. Instances of meritorious conduct. Statesmanlike utterances. In other words, the Washington Monument.

Is the explanation that Washington really was a paragon? Was he stainless, as so many writers would have us believe? Or did he merely represent conscientious mediocrity, placed in power and automatically hallowed because he was the instrument of victory? Did Americans revere him because by circumstance he came to stand for everything they held dear?

Did they turn him into a monument because in the early days of the Republic he was all that they had in the way of a national symbol or entity? If so, how much was he aware of the process and how much did he lend himself to it?

These are few of the conundrums that tease us. It may be possible to hint at some answers in the final chapter of this book. In the next three chapters, however, we must struggle to forget about the Washington Monument. Ideally we should pretend that we have never even heard of Washington, or that the American colonies revolted against Britain and formed an independent nation. If this is too much to expect, we should at least keep reminding ourselves that these things were hidden from Washington. Looking back on the events of Washington's life, some of his panegyrists have discovered Providence busily at work. Here and here, they say, are proofs that it was all foreordained; so shapely and illustrious an outcome *must* have been. Washington himself frequently spoke of destiny, and committed himself to it. But he did so in no

Napoleonic mood. He never felt that he was the Man of Destiny, only that what would be would be. When he ventured to predict, he usually did so by way of warning: such or such would be the melancholy consequences, if Americans failed to guard against them. If he seemed to walk confidently, he walked into the dark, without benefit of second sight – a mortal man in an ennobling but bewildering time, for whom tomorrow was a problem and next year an enigma. This is what we must remember about him. In his own eyes, history happened to him, not the other way round. He did what he could.

CHAPTER TWO

GEORGE WASHINGTON, ESQUIRE

Where's his bright ploughshare that he loved – or his wheat-crowned fields, waving in yellow ridges before the wanton breeze – or his hills whitened over with flocks – or his clover-coloured pastures spread with innumerous herds – or his neat-clad servants, with songs rolling the heavy harvest before them? Such were the scenes of peace, plenty, and happiness, in which Washington delighted.

MASON WEEMS, *The Life of George Washington;*
with curious anecdotes, equally honourable to himself
and exemplary to his young countrymen.

Virginia Origins

As in a film projected in reverse, we demolish the monument. The plinths and statues disappear; the wings of the mansion at Mount Vernon are whirled away, and the portico, the dove-shaped weathervane, the furnishings, and then the very core of the house and its foundations, leaving no trace. The roads are peeled from the surface of the land; the farms and inns and churches and courthouses are scraped off. Old tree stumps shoot up again into branches, trunk and leaves, then dwindle backward to sapling, to seed. The Indians and the buffalo they hunted are once more found along the seaboard. Like iron filings answering a magnet, the ships are drawn in, stern first, eastward across the Atlantic; their cargoes are magicked from the holds, their living freight of settlers, servants, convicts and slaves disgorged. The sun climbs in the west from darkness to sunset, rises to high noon, and falls toward the eastern dawn. . . .

We may arrest this process of undoing in the 1650s, when the first Washingtons came to Virginia. The earliest British settlers had arrived there half a century before, at Jamestown. Despite sickness, famine, Indian wars and changes of government, settlements gradually spread along the coastal promontories and up the rivers — Potomac, Rappahannock, York and James, as they lay from north to south. At home in Britain the Stuart king Charles I was overthrown in the Civil War, and beheaded. A royal colony, Virginia first espoused the Stuart cause, only to be compelled to recognize the rule of Parliament. To outward appearance, the change did not make much difference in Virginia. In that "infant, woody country" (as George Washington could still describe it a century later) food, shelter, protection and land were more immediately important.

But what happened at home was also important sooner or later to Virginia. One event that had large consequences was the granting by Charles II to a faithful follower (in 1649 — only a few months after his father's death) of an enormous tract of territory in the Northern Neck between the Potomac and the Rappahannock. It seemed a pathetic gesture, in that young Charles was then in exile, with dubious prospects of ever enforcing his decrees. He had given away a fortune he did not possess and that neither he nor the new "Proprietor" had ever seen or was ever to see.

Another small incident of the Civil War in England — typical of what befell thousands of unlucky men — was the expulsion from his living of an Anglican minister by the Puritans in 1643. His name was

Lawrence Washington. He had lived in modest comfort (his family had owned the manor of Sulgrave, in Northamptonshire, and he himself was a former Fellow of Brasenose College, Oxford). Now he found survival difficult; and after he died in 1653, two of his sons decided to make a fresh start in Virginia. One of them, John, came as a ship's officer, married the daughter of a Virginia landowner and – perhaps half by accident – settled there. In general he prospered. He acquired land; he became a justice of the peace and a burgess (i.e., a member of the lower house of the Virginia General Assembly). His brother was also reasonably successful. The Washington line was established. It could hardly be called a dynasty, as yet. Neither brother made a fortune. Life was precarious and rough, death ever-present. John, for example, had three wives, the last of whom had already been widowed three times, and he was still only in his middle forties when he died in 1677.

Nevertheless, the Washington name quietly joined those others – Byrd, Carter, Corbin, Fitzhugh, Harrison, Lee, Page, Randolph – that we associate with Virginia. John's eldest son, Lawrence, carried on the line, benefiting as elder sons did from the rules of inheritance that were to characterize the colony. Lawrence too was a burgess; but he died in 1698, at the age of thirty-nine, before he was able to fasten much grip upon his surroundings. And now the story wanders into a maze of inheritances, land claims, intermarriage and litigation – the complex of so much of colonial Virginia's history. Lawrence's children were taken to England by their mother, who, according to the custom of the time, promptly remarried. The two boys in the family were sent to school at Appleby in Westmoreland. Their stepfather might have kept them in England, and their Virginia properties might have been lost to them. However, their mother soon died and they came back to Virginia. The legal tangle involving their lands was gradually simplified. One of the sons, Augustine, was about twenty-one (the average age for matrimony among Virginia males) when he took Jane Butler as his wife, in about 1715. The first surviving son of this marriage was christened Lawrence, after his grandfather and great-great-grandfather.

Augustine worked hard and showed some enterprise. Like his father and grandfather, he was a county justice. With his own and his wife's property, he had title to 1750 acres in various parts of the Northern Neck. In 1726 he also acquired rights to 2,500 acres of the Little Hunting Creek tract on the Potomac, which had been patented by his settler grandfather, John. And he secured an interest in an iron furnace.

In 1729 Augustine's wife died. Two years later – a relatively long interval for those days – he married again. His second wife was Mary

Ball, an orphan of twenty-three with a middling property and the usual circle of relatives. She was descended from a William Ball, the son of a London attorney who came to Virginia in 1650. Mary was much attached to her guardian, a genial lawyer named George Eskridge; and it was apparently after him that she named her first-born child: George Washington. Otherwise he might perhaps have been given the family name of John; Lawrence and Augustine had already been used for his half brothers. At any rate, George it was.

The baby George was born in Westmoreland County, at a plantation later known as Wakefield. It was also described as Pope's Creek or Bridges' Creek, since it lay between those two streams, which emptied into the Potomac some way down river from the Hunting Creek property. George's birth date was February 11, 1732. (When the calendar was revised in 1752, eleven days were added, so that this date subsequently became February 22, New Style.) Five other children came in rapid succession: Elizabeth, Samuel, John Augustine, Charles and Mildred, who died in infancy in 1740.

By then young George was living in his third home. In 1735 his father had moved to Prince William County. Three years later he moved again, to Ferry Farm near the little settlement of Fredericksburg on the Rappahannock. The father had worries and disappointments, especially with his iron foundry, but he was fairly well entrenched as a Virginian of the upper, though not the top, level. He owned about fifty slaves. He acquired title to all the lands he could encompass: something over ten thousand acres, as enumerated in his will. He sent Lawrence and Augustine, the two sons of his first marriage, to the school he had himself attended, at Appleby in northern England. Thus might they acquire the breadth and polish befitting a Virginia gentleman; through luck, shrewd investment and a careful marriage they might amass the wealth to accompany such manners.

Then, however, the picture changed. When George was just eleven years old, father Augustine died. Most of his property was left to the half brothers, Lawrence and Augustine. George was to inherit Ferry Farm when he came of age. In the meantime he lived there with his mother, leaving childhood behind and entering the short period of youth that in colonial times so swiftly merged with adult life. The events of his childhood can only be guessed at – unless we care to accept the picturesque anecdotes of Parson Weems and others. One common story is that he was taught to read and write by "a convict servant whom his father brought over as a schoolteacher." That is possible: convicts as well as indentured servants were dispatched to Virginia in considerable numbers; and some convicts were no doubt educated men whose offenses had not been particularly heinous. But there is no proof of this story. Nor is there any certainty, though it sounds more likely, that George attended a school in Fredericksburg – the one conducted by the Rev. James Marye. All we can assume is that George got some schooling between the ages of seven and eleven. There is no mention of any idea of sending him to Appleby, perhaps because this would have been too expensive and perhaps because his mother did not want to be separated from him for several years, which this would have entailed. Whatever the cause, his schooling was provincial in several ways.

After his father's death George evidently continued to absorb instruction of a sort. The adolescent notebooks which have survived show that he learned some elementary Latin and mathematics, picked up the rudiments of good conduct, and read a little in English literature. By European standards it was a sketchy education for a gentleman, and it was all the formal education he was to have, since, unlike some of his contemporaries, he did not go on to the College of William and Mary, in the Virginia capital at Williamsburg. We do not know why, unless again his mother's frugality and desire to keep him close at hand are the explanation. In short, George Washington was not highly educated, and never became what might be called an intellectual. Here he is in sharp contrast with Americans like John Adams, who was later to maintain, sourly, "That Washington was not a scholar is certain. That he was too illiterate, unlearned, unread for his station and reputation is equally past dispute."

Nor, of course, does he compare in intellectual preparation and power with such Virginia contemporaries as Thomas Jefferson and James Madison. Years afterward Washington probably felt the lack. He was ill at ease in set debate or abstract discussion. He managed to express himself on paper with a degree of clarity and force, through long practice, and his spelling likewise improved, but he was never a brilliant writer.[5] We may attribute a little of the constraint of the mature Washington to his awareness of his own intellectual limitations. While still a young man, he was to suffer through his ignorance of the French language, and afterwards he was to refuse an invitation to visit France, on the grounds that he would be embarrassed by having to converse

[5] The Rules of Civility, from an early notebook, are sometimes listed among Washington's own writings but were merely copied down by him (" . . . In speaking to men of Quality do not lean nor Look them full in the Face, Nor approach too near them at least. Keep a full pace from them . . ."). As for the compositions of his mature years, their ideas came from Washington, but their phraseology – since he was an extremely busy man – had often to be left to his secretaries. Some of the latter wrote with considerable polish.

through an interpreter. Unlike Jefferson and Adams, he never did reach Europe.

But we must not overstress this point. In Virginia, the intellectual attainment of a Jefferson or a Madison was exceptional. Even the wealthiest planters tended not to be bookish, or particularly concerned with cultural refinements. William Byrd of Westover, with his library of perhaps three thousand volumes, was unique among the gentry of tidewater Virginia. They lived comfortably, somewhat on the lines of the English squirearchy, fond of food and drink, good imported clothes and well-made imported furniture. But their lives had less of civilized elegance than some chroniclers have suggested. Their homes were surprisingly small, in most instances; their broad acres seemed (to European eyes) shaggy and unkempt – very near to the wilderness in both time and space. By trade and sentiment they were close to the mother country; even their speech sounded much nearer to the mother tongue than did the nasal utterance of Massachusetts (though it was said that their children were too readily allowed to pick up the slurred speech of the Negro slaves). But in other respects the Virginia of the mid-eighteenth century was a world on its own, far removed from Europe or from the patterns of urban civilization. Young Washington once referred jokingly to Williamsburg as "the great Metropolis." In comparison with Boston or Philadelphia (let alone London, which Washington also described in the same phrase), Williamsburg was a small town. And Williamsburg, Yorktown, Hampton and Norfolk formed the only sizable townships in Virginia at that period, though others were growing up. Virginia was a rural colony, with rural tastes. It was also a large and proud colony, but its units of existence – plantation, parish, county – were local. Burgesses who attended the Assembly at Williamsburg enjoyed a brief and hectic round of town life, of dances, dinners, card games and theater parties. Otherwise the Virginia planter – not to mention the humbler farmers, who made up the bulk of the population – was a countryman, a busy squire and local potentate.

His absorbing interest was land. The average planter owned several tracts. One estate he might farm himself, with tobacco as the staple crop; others might be let to tenants; and others again, in the western areas, might be uncleared and untenanted (unless invaded by squatters). His fortune was based on land; his future and that of his family depended upon the acquisition of still more land. The great men of Virginia – men like Robert Carter of Nomini – reckoned their wealth in tens of thousands of acres. The gold fever that lured the hopeful to California and hundred years hence was a swift and consuming passion. The land fever of colonial Virginia was less ephemeral but hardly less intense in its effects. And no wonder, when so much land lay to the west, with only the Indians and the French to dispute possession – except for one's rivals in Virginia (or in Maryland and Pennsylvania).

The Virginian's love of land was sometimes lavish and careless. He farmed as well as he knew how, yet without the minute economy of the European peasant. If tobacco exhausted the fertility of his soil, as it did, he was sorry; but there was always another estate to be made elsewhere from fresh ground. This, then, was the Virginian's dream – a litigious, competitive, restless dream, beset with warnings, disasters and vulgarities, yet nevertheless a kind of ideal. "Speculation" in its original sense meant, deep thought upon some abstract problem. In a newer sense (of which the first use, according to the *Oxford Dictionary,* was in 1774) it meant "engagement in any business enterprise or transaction of a venturesome or risky nature, but offering the chance of great . . . gain." This is a fairly apt description of the outlook of the alert Virginia planter. It did not exclude the consideration of more fundamental problems, as and when the need should arise. Every speculator knew how to argue and protest.

The planter's diversions followed naturally from his workaday life. He made a pleasure of the necessity of long hours on horseback. "My dear countrymen," said Colonel William Byrd, "have so great a passion for riding that they will often walk two miles to catch a horse to ride one." The planter liked to watch (and bet on) horse races, to hunt foxes and shoot game. Occasionally, in more brutal fashion, he wagered money on cockfighting. It was a robust and rather violent existence, and bred a certain callousness in those who led it, as well as a good deal of courage. Here, as in other colonies, bounties were offered for Indian scalps. The penal code, though no harsher than that of England in most instances, could be summary – especially for Negroes, who might for graver crimes be hung and quartered, or even burned alive.

VIRGINIA INFLUENCES

This was the young Washington's Virginia, and his education was well enough devised to meet its demands. He became a fair marksman and a fine horseman – by common consent, one of the best of his age. He grew tall, strong and active. George did not, however, run wild. True, there is nothing to show a refining influence on his mother's part. Despite the glowing tributes that have been paid to her, she seems to have been a narrow, grudging, unimaginative woman; and in later years it is clear that George showed her respect but could not add to it much warmth of affection. Her only positive action with the adolescent boy appears to have been to forbid – perhaps quite sensibly – a scheme to send him to sea as a midshipman.

But fortunately there were other influences in the family, and in particular that of his half-brother Lawrence. Lawrence was fourteen years older than George, and a genuine friend. Schooled in England, he no doubt seemed an attractive and worldly figure, a welcome substitute for the father George had lost. When George was a boy of eight, Lawrence went off to the West Indies as a captain (one of four Virginians thus honored) in the newly raised American Regiment, to take part in Admiral Vernon's expedition against the Spanish at Cartagena. Through no fault of the Admiral's the exploit was a costly failure. Many of the American Regiment died of yellow fever. Lawrence came home in advance of the other survivors, to retire from service on half pay. He applied for, and later occupied, the post of adjutant general for Virginia. Here, if we are looking for formative influence upon the young Washington, is an obvious, military one. His half brother, while denied military glory, had at any rate acquitted himself properly in what could have been a tremendous adventure. As for Lawrence, he so admired the Admiral that he named his estate at Hunting Creek Mount Vernon, and hung a portrait of the Admiral in the house he built there.

A second influence supplied by Lawrence could be called social. In 1743, the year of their father's death, Lawrence made a most desirable match. His bride was Anne Fairfax, the daughter of the prosperous Colonel William Fairfax of Belvoir, an estate almost adjacent to Mount Vernon. Colonel Fairfax was a grandee in Virginia; and soon after the wedding he proved the fact by joining the exclusive Council (or upper house of the Virginia General Assembly), a body composed of the twelve leading dignitaries of the colony. Through Lawrence the Fairfaxes were to play an important part in shaping the development of George. When he was sixteen or thereabouts he came to live mainly at Mount Vernon. He learned to play billiards, whist and loo; he was taught to dance; and he began, half in jest and half in agonizing earnest, to pay attention to girls. His letters and journals allude wistfully-facetiously to a "Low Land Beauty" and other distracting creatures. Biographers have lingered over these references, and over the circumstances of an unsuccessful infatuation with one Betsy Fauntleroy when he was twenty. Such allusions do have a curious fascination, partly because they show young Washington as a vulnerable human being and partly because the figures involved are so shadowy. Yet they provide too little evidence to clinch the contention that George was exceptionally awkward in drawing-room encounters. Perhaps he was a little heavy and humorless, as well as immature; was he much different from his local rivals? We can only guess at the truth.

A related and more tantalizing conundrum is offered by Sarah (Sally) Cary, the daughter of Colonel Wilson Cary, who had an estate on the James River near Hampton. In December 1748, at eighteen, she married George William, the eldest son of Colonel Fairfax, and made Belvoir her home. Her husband was an agreeable young man whom George Washington could count on as a friend, though a few months earlier he had referred to him politely in a diary as Mr. Fairfax. For years to come George was to see much of Sally, to write to her now and then – and perhaps to fall in love with her. It seems certain, from his letters to her, that he liked her very much, valued her friendship, and yet was not entirely at ease with her. From her few letters to him it would appear that Sally enjoyed admiration and recognized no sharp dividing line between badinage and flirtation. Was he, then, in love with her? Again, the evidence is too fragmentary for us to tell. If he was, we can be virtually certain that the relationship remained a matter of sentiment and private hurt.

At any rate, she and young Fairfax and Lawrence and Ann Fairfax gave George a glimpse of a delightful and privileged existence. If his behavior *was* a shade awkward, he was, after all, young, without a father, becoming like a stepson to these two couples. He had useful connections, and he was not penniless; he was not cast in the role of Cinderella with Lawrence and Augustine as the ugly sisters. But he must have realized that he had to shift for himself, or at least take advantage of all opportunities that came his way. Ultimately and accidentally his situation was well contrived to bring him on. By comparison, the Fairfax children were a little spoiled, as George's own stepson and stepson's children were to be.[6] He, on the other hand, could understand the pinch of deprivation if he had never actually felt it. His ambition was sharpened, therefore, instead of smothered. Hence this sort of advice, which he pressed upon one of his own younger brothers in 1755:

> I shou'd be glad to hear you live [in] Harmony and good
> fellowship with the family at Belvoir, as it is in their power to
> be very serviceable upon many occasion's to us, as young

[6] "I never did in my life," a tutor commented on Washington's stepson Jack, "know a youth so exceedingly indolent or so surprisingly voluptuous: one would suppose Nature had intended him for some Asiatic Prince."

beginner's. I would advise your visiting often as one step towards it.

The third influence upon the young beginner George that came from Lawrence and the Fairfaxes could be labeled territorial. In 1750 one Virginia leader reminded the Board of Trade at home that his colony's western claims stretched as far as "the South Sea" (the Pacific Ocean), "including California." It was a vast claim – and a vague one, when we recall that a few years earlier young George had in a school copybook listed "Colofornia" as one of the "Chief Islands" of North America, together with "Icelands," "Greenland," "Barbadoes and the rest of the Caribee Islands," and so on. Less vaguely, every aspiring Virginian knew that to the west lay the Blue Ridge Mountains. Beyond them was the rich valley of the Shenandoah, and parallel was the barrier of the Alleghenies. To the northwest of the lower Shenandoah was debatable ground: The Ohio Valley, which in turn led to the great basin of the Mississippi. It was all a rich prize, for himself or for his children and their children; and the colonist had no intention of relinquishing it. He pressed his case by every means. In 1744, by a treaty between Virginia, Maryland and the Indians of the Iroquois confederation, the western boundary of white settlement was agreed to be the Alleghenies, and not – as previously maintained by the Indians – the Blue Ridge. The Shenandoah Valley was thus opened to settlement. And a few months later the Privy Council in London reached a decision on a matter that harked back to the frail, ninety-year-old promise of Charles II. Charles *had* succeeded to the throne, and his lucky follower *had* become Proprietor of the Northern Neck. In 1744, through inheritance, the Proprietor was Thomas Lord Fairfax; and the Privy Council decided a long dispute over rights and boundaries in his favor. The extent of his domain was re-defined so as to take in a large area between the upper Potomac and Rappahannock.

Lord Fairfax was the cousin of Colonel Fairfax, who had been acting as his agent and had gained much power thereby. The Proprietor was a dull, suspicious-minded man who did less to help George than is sometimes alleged. But he was an almost legendary figure, and we may picture the excitement he aroused when in 1748 he came out to Virginia to see his possessions. He took up residence to begin with at Belvoir. By then Lawrence and other speculators had formed the Ohio Company, in order to develop an enormous land grant in the region of the Upper Potomac. The frontier was on the move; indeed, an even more ambitious development scheme – the Loyal Company – was initiated by another group of venturers at the same time.

The connection between these grandiose territorial projects and the first career of young Washington is obvious. Land was important; Washington became a surveyor. Perhaps Lawrence was partly responsible; if he was kind to George, he did not train him to be a dandy. Lawrence may have suggested sending George to sea, which was not an elegant career or (as George's uncle pointed out) one with much chance of "preferment." Still, there is no need to find elaborate explanations. Probably every Virginia planter learned something about surveying, and was taught as a boy – as George was – how to draft a bill of sale, a power of attorney, a promissory note.

When George was sixteen he knew enough about surveying to assist in running lines. He did this in 1748, when he accompanied a Fairfax party to the Shenandoah country – his first trip across the Blue Ridge. Next year he was employed as assistant surveyor in laying out the new town of Belhaven (rechristened Alexandria) on the Potomac a few miles north of Mount Vernon. Lawrence Washington was one of the trustees of Alexandria; so George was launching himself under family auspices. Soon after, he was appointed surveyor of Culpeper County. And now, on a modest scale, his career advanced briskly as he carried out surveys throughout the newer areas of northern Virginia. By the end of 1750 the eighteen-year-old surveyor had even managed to lay claim on his own behalf to three tracts – of 1,450 acres altogether – in the lower Shenandoah. Since Ferry Farm would soon come into his hands, he could view his prospects with some satisfaction. If he was not an intellectual genius, or the heir to a great fortune, he was evidently energetic, reliable – and canny.

At the end of 1751 there came a break in his steady routine. Lawrence Washington's first three children had died, and he himself was troubled by a cough that grew steadily worse. Medical treatment was haphazard and unavailing. In desperation he decided to make a voyage to Barbados, in the hope that the mild climate would cure him. Lawrence's wife had to stay behind with their fourth infant, so George went with Lawrence (his only journey outside what was to be the continental United States). The experiment failed, Lawrence's health remained poor, and George succumbed to smallpox. When George recovered, he returned alone to Virginia with the cheerless news that Lawrence was worse, if anything, and would probably move on to Bermuda in further search of a remedy. Meanwhile George resumed his existence as a surveyor. He bought another Shenandoah tract, which brought his holding there to two thousand acres.

Otherwise 1752 was a gloomy year. George fell ill with pleurisy; he had no luck with Miss Fauntleroy; and Lawrence came back that summer from Bermuda, to die of tuberculosis. Death seemed to mock at human pretensions. Yet there were unlooked-for consolations in the shape of Lawrence's bequests, and opportunities to follow in the directions Lawrence had indicated. By the terms of his brother's will the widow was to enjoy the use of Mount Vernon during her lifetime, in trust for the sole remaining child; but if this child died without issue, Mount Vernon was to pass to George. He was to have Lawrence's other property in Fairfax County when the widow died. It was a generous will as far as George was concerned, the more so in that the Fairfax baby soon joined the others in the grave. Moreover, Lawrence's death left open the militia adjutancy of Virginia. George applied for and got one of the four adjutancies into which the colony was subsequently divided.

As he came of age in 1753 young Washington was soundly placed. He had just been enrolled as a Freemason in the new lodge at Fredericksburg; he was a county surveyor, with an annual stipend of fifty pounds and a remunerative practice; apart from his two thousand Shenandoah acres, he had inherited altogether another four thousand; and as a district adjutant he drew a salary of one hundred pounds a year, with the militia rank of major. Before long, instead of making Ferry Farm his seat, he leased Mount Vernon from his sister-in-law. Henceforward it was his home; eventually he owned it outright, and for more than forty years it was to lie at the center of his own private vision. To complete his domestic security, all that he needed was a wife.

THE YOUNG SOLDIER

But for a while this quest was deferred. The youthful planter became immersed in another vision – of military prowess. This episode of Washington's life lasted five years. It is worth dwelling upon in some detail. Let us, to begin with, summarize the main features of his early military career as a kind of success story. We may then, a little less superficially, notice their significance as a commentary upon his character and aspirations.

In 1753 Britain's colonial empire in North America lay along the eastern seaboard, up to the line of the Alleghenies. The American empire of France, with whom Britain had been intermittently at war for half a century, ran to the north and west in a huge encircling arc, but if France strengthened her hold, Virginia and the other colonies would be confined to their coastal belt. If, on the other hand, Britain seized the Ohio valley, the arc could be broken and even the Mississippi could be wrested from the French. Virginia, and more especially the Ohio Company, was intimately involved in the clash. In theory the two nations had been at peace since 1748. In reality, trouble was imminent, for there was no peace but only an armed truce. The Ohio Company determined to build a fort at the forks of the Ohio, where the Monongahela and the Allegheny rivers came together. Their scouts, however, reported that the French were constructing a chain of rival forts – Presque Isle, Le Boeuf and perhaps Venango and Logstown – southward from Lake Erie to the Ohio. Robert Dinwiddie, the lieutenant governor of Virginia, delivered an ultimatum, and Major Washington carried it.

Bearing a polite but adamant letter from Dinwiddie to the French commander in the area, Washington set off along the Potomac in October 1753. On the way he picked up an able frontiersman named Christopher Gist, a Dutchman called Van Braam (to act as interpreter – Van Braam understood French) and four other men. Two and a half months later Washington arrived back in Williamsburg with an equally polite but no less adamant reply from Fort Le Boeuf.

It had been a hard journey, in wretched weather. The party traveled by canoe and on horseback, at first on the new Ohio Company trail that Gist had been clearing, and then through wilderness. They crossed the Potomac watershed to the Youghiogheny valley, thence to the point where the Youghiogheny flowed into the Monongahela, on to Shannopin's Town (an Indian settlement close by the Ohio forks), on to Logstown, Venango and so to Le Boeuf, almost to the shore of Lake Erie. Everything was new to Washington – the wild and broken terrain, the devious ways of the Indians, the bland but stubborn French who "told me, That it was their absolute Design to take possession of the Ohio, and by G——— they would do it." When he was at last able to leave, in a desperate hurry to convey the disquieting news, Washington pushed ahead with Gist. They endured extreme hardship and danger. An Indian shot at them from almost point-blank range (fortunately he missed); to throw him off the trail, they traveled all night, after pretending to pitch camp, then all the next day. They had to build a raft in order to cross the half-frozen Allegheny. George was knocked overboard and nearly drowned, and spent a miserably cold night in sodden clothing. Oddly enough, though, it was Gist and not George that got frostbite.

Back at length in Williamsburg, he rapidly wrote out an account of the journey at Dinwiddie's request. Dinwiddie had the narrative printed, no doubt to impress the Assembly with the seriousness of the situation, and it was reprinted in London in three different publications with due credit given to Washington. The Assembly was in fact impressed enough to vote him fifty pounds. He had a new patron in Dinwiddie, who, according to legend, commended him as a "braw laddie." Major Washington's star was in the ascendant.

What followed seemed to prove that destiny had marked him out. Dinwiddie planned an expedition to hold the Ohio country, and Washington was chosen as its second-in-command with a lieutenant colonel's commission in the Virginia militia. While Washington was recruiting his force, Gist and another agent of the Ohio Company – William Trent – were busy on the frontier, building a company warehouse on the Monongahela and a company fort at the forks of the Ohio. Trent was given a captain's commission and told to recruit a company of frontiersmen. Lieutenant Colonel Washington was instructed to reinforce Trent with two more companies.

He set out on this mission in April 1754, from Alexandria. With him were eight subordinate officers (including Van Braam, for whom Washington had procured a captaincy), a surgeon, "a Swedish gentleman volunteer" and one hundred fifty men. A three-week march brought his command to Wills Creek on the upper Potomac (later the site of Fort Cumberland). Here an alarming rumor was confirmed: Trent had been ousted from the Ohio forks by a far superior French force and was withdrawing toward Wills Creek. However, the neighboring Indians affirmed their loyalty. Encouraged by their fidelity, and eager to prove himself, Washington agreed with his officers that they should continue on as far as the Monongahela warehouse. They would then be less than forty miles from the Ohio forks, the strategic place at which the French in turn were at work on a fort that they called Duquesne.

The advance to the Monongahela went slowly, through wild and broken country which his wagon train could hardly penetrate. In a period of fifteen days he was able to cover only twenty miles. But he pushed forward, through the Great Meadows to Laurel Mountain, where Gist returned from a reconnaissance with the information that a French party was hiding nearby. Early next morning Washington came to grips with them. Who fired first cannot be stated. No one should have fired, since the two countries were not formally at war. But they were so close to war that the point has little relevance. The facts are that Washington's men took the French by surprise and routed them in a brief skirmish, killing ten and taking twenty more as prisoners. The French leader, M. de Jumonville, was among the slain, several of whom were scalped by Washington's Indians. His own losses were slight: one man killed and two or three wounded.

This was at the end of May. Washington forwarded the prisoners to Virginia. His actions met with approval; and as his commander had died, Washington was made a full colonel in charge of the whole Virginia contingent, though not of the companies promised from other colonies. Only one of these actually arrived in time to make any difference. But by the close of June 1754 Colonel Washington was responsible for a miscellaneous band of Virginia militia, North Carolina regulars and Indian tribesmen.

He now got word that a much stronger French force was at Fort Duquesne, about to attack him. Short of provisions, gradually deserted by his Indians and harassed by other problems, Washington drew his troops into a hastily improvised stockade at Great Meadows which he named Fort Necessity. On July 3, by which time all his Indians had melted away, the French surrounded the fort. Unlike the Jumonville skirmish, this fight lasted most of the day, in drenching rain. The French kept up a heavy fire, working nearer and nearer. Fort Necessity provided poor protection; Washington's men suffered serious losses, while all their cattle and horses were shot dead by the French. The colonists' position was hopeless; with little food or ammunition left, they were outnumbered and trapped. Washington was compelled to give in. The French allowed him to march out under arms and to take his force back to Virginia, except for two officer hostages. One of these was Van Braam, who, still acting as interpreter, translated the instrument of surrender that the French required him to sign.

It was a bitter defeat for the young officer. Some thought he had shown poor judgment. But he had done his best, and in general his actions were praised, both at Williamsburg and in London. For a comparative youngster he was famous; a private letter of his describing the Jumonville skirmish was reprinted in the *London Magazine*, and Horace Walpole ways that he spoke about it with King George II. "We obtained a most signal victory," Washington had written to his brother, adding with youthful enthusiasm, "I heard the bullets whistle, and, believe me, there is something charming in the sound." According to Walpole, King George remarked that Washington "would not say so, had he heard many." This wry comment was unknown at the time to Washington or his Virginia contemporaries. But he knew that what was happening in the back country was under keen scrutiny in Paris and London. It was intoxicating for a young provincial soldier to think that the local event, of his own producing, held world-wide significance.

Indeed, Washington became for a brief period a figure of notoriety when the French published his personal journal, which by accident was left behind at Fort Necessity. They used it for propaganda purposes, so as to prove that the British were the aggressors in these frontier clashes. Jumonville, they maintained, had come on a peaceful errand much like Washington's mission a few months earlier, only to be "assassinated." Since Van Braam had failed to notice the ugly word in the surrender document, where it occurred more than once, the French contended that Washington had signed an admission of his own guilt. Yet though the French spoke of him as an archvillain, and even featured him as such in a long epic poem composed for the occasion, this was all the more reason for British fellow countrymen to defend him, pointing out that he had signed in haste and virtually under duress. Nor, certainly, was it his fault that the Virginia authorities dishonored his pledge, in the Fort Necessity agreement, to arrange the release of the prisoners captured in the Jumonville encounter.

Gradually the fuss died down, and several months went by before Washington was again embroiled. He resigned his commission in 1754, in despair at the confusion that seemed to attend all plans connected with frontier campaigning. But in the spring of 1755 he once more took the familiar route toward the Ohio forks. This time he was a volunteer, without official status, like the "Swedish gentleman" who had marched with him a year before. The opportunity, though, was promising. General Edward Braddock, a senior soldier of decided views, had arrived in Virginia with two British regular battalions to clear away the French from that part of British America and Washington secured an invitation to act as an unpaid member of Braddock's "family" of aides-de-camp.

As usual there were tiresome delays. Finally at the end of May 1755, Braddock's army (of something over two thousand men, in regulars, volunteers and militia) was setting out from Fort Cumberland to cover the one hundred fifty miles to Fort Duquesne. Burdened by baggage and artillery, the force moved so slowly that — at his own suggestion, Washington says — the less mobile elements traveled separately in the rear. He was with them, suffering from an attack of dysentery, when six weeks later the bullets began to whistle in a less charming way.

Braddock's advance guard was within a few miles of Duquesne, probing cautiously through the woods, when it was rushed by a band of French and Indians. Clad in Indian costume, and led by a bold French officer, they appeared suddenly among the trees, spread out at his signal and opened fire. For a little while the British had the situation in control, and the French attack wavered. Then the balance of the battle swung against Braddock. Bunched in their conspicuous clothing, bewildered by accurate fire from unseen enemies, unable to get into formation and fight as they were trained to do, the British redcoats gradually became a mass of helpless, frantic men, dropping in scores. Struggling to rally the ranks, nearly three quarters of their officers became casualties. Braddock, among them, bursting with angry courage as he rode to and fro on horseback, was mortally wounded. The Virginia troops behaved more coolly, according to Washington, who hastened up to join in the contest. His own efforts and those of others were unavailing. Indeed, he was lucky to escape with his life; two horses were shot under him, and his clothing torn by bullets. Many were less lucky. The woods became a slaughter ground. Close on nine hundred of Braddock's men lay dead or wounded, a harvest of scalps for the yelling Indians ("The terrific sound" of their whoops "will haunt me till the hour of my dissolution," said a British officer afterwards) as the demoralized survivors poured back in retreat.

The disaster might still have been amended if Braddock's second-in-command had gathered the remnants and again advanced on Duquesne. In fact, the battle might easily have gone the other way. Braddock was not as foolish as tradition alleges: his men were not taken completely by surprise; he outnumbered the French; and if the sortie from Duquesne had been less audacious, it would have failed. Yet these postmortem reflections could not alter the shameful reality of defeat. Duquesne was still French, and the whole Virginia frontier lay exposed to marauding Indians, jubilant with victory.

There was some comfort for Washington. Whatever the general dismay and recrimination, his own reputation did not suffer. He was known to have behaved gallantly, although a sick man. "Permit me now Sir," the governor of North Carolina wrote, "to congratulate you on Your Late Escape and the Immortal Honour You have Gain'd on the Banks of the Ohio," and he received other equally complimentary letters. He returned to Virginia's service, again as a colonel, but now with the title of Commander in Chief of Virginia's soldiery. This was in August 1755, when he was only twenty-three.

The title was exalted, the task sickeningly hard. With a few hundred men he was supposed to protect a three-hundred-fifty-mile line. The high hopes of settler and speculator alike seemed shattered. War was not officially declared between Britain and France until May 1756; and both before and after that date the main campaigns were staged elsewhere in North America. Washington and his companions in the western outposts began to feel that they were forgotten men on a forgotten front. In the latter part of 1757 he fell ill again with dysentery. Finally he had to give up, gravely unwell, and come home to Mount

Vernon, doomed perhaps to follow his father and his half brother to the graveyard. Still unmarried, he had not even a direct heir to continue his line. Mount Vernon had been sadly neglected; so had his other affairs. He had twice put his name forward as a burgess at election time, and had twice been vanquished at the polls.

Yet with the spring of 1758 he was fit again and ready to engage in another campaign. A British army under Brigadier General Forbes – one of several in North America – was again to advance on Fort Duquesne. It would be the fourth time that Washington had taken that trail. But to his horror and indignation, Forbes decided not to follow the well-worn path but to cut a new road westward from Raystown in Pennsylvania. In vain Washington pleaded the merits of his route; Forbes had the last word. So – as Washington saw it, in despair of the outcome – the weeks dragged into months, till the summer was gone and Forbes's army was still hacking its way toward the Ohio forks. The British had almost decided to abandon their effort for the winter when, at the end of November 1758, the French finally relinquished the struggle in the Ohio valley, leaving Fort Duquesne in flames without waiting for a siege. There was a rather dreary element of anticlimax in this bloodless success. Yet the desired result had been achieved. Fort Pitt, now a British stronghold, rose on the ashes of Duquesne, and a measure of tranquility returned to the Virginia frontier.

Washington was ready to say a personal farewell to arms, though elsewhere the struggle against France continued. He had ended the campaign with the honorary rank of brigadier; in 1758 he had at last been victorious as candidate for the House of Burgesses in Frederick County; and he was engaged to be married. When they heard of his impending resignation, the officers of his Virginia Regiment, urging him to stay another year, said in a "Humble Address":

> Judge then, how sensibly we must be Affected with the loss of such an excellent Commander, such a sincere Friend, and so affable a Companion. . . .

> It gives us an additional Sorrow, when we reflect, to find, our unhappy Country will receive a loss, no less irreparable, than ourselves. Where will it meet a Man so experienc'd in military Affairs? One so renown'd for Patriotism, Courage and Conduct? . . . In you we place the most implicit Confidence. Your Presence only will cause a steady Firmness and Vigor to actuate in every Breast, despising the greatest Dangers, and thinking

light of Toils and Hardships, while lead on by the Man we know and Love.

There was no doubting the genuineness of such a tribute. Nor can we overlook the essential truth of his own statement to Dinwiddie (in September 1757):

> That I have foibles, and perhaps many of them, I shall not deny. I should esteem myself, as the world also would, vain and empty, were I to arrogate perfection . . . but this I know, and it is the highest consolation I am capable of feeling, that no man, that was ever employed in a public capacity, has endeavoured to discharge the trust reposed in him with greater honesty and more zeal for the country's interest, than I have done.

Yet there is something a little odd in this declaration, something that needs further examination before we take up the story of Colonel Washington in retirement. In conjunction with Washington's other correspondence of this five-year period, it reminds us that to him they were mainly years of frustration and humiliation. Nor can we blame him for being exasperated at times. As his officers assured him, he came to know the forms and possibilities of frontier warfare as thoroughly as anyone in the colony – and a great deal better than most of the legislators in far-off Williamsburg. He was eager to oust the French before they grew too strong and won over all the Indians in the Ohio country. But he met with maddening obstacles. The Assembly seemed to him blind to "the country's interest"; one burgess even said that the French had a right to the Ohio. Suspicious of Dinwiddie (and of the Ohio Company, with which the Governor was associated), the Assembly was reluctant to vote funds. Dinwiddie, though not apathetic, was apt to be parsimonious (at least, as George viewed him). Nursing private plans, he was unhelpful in other respects. He became less and less friendly to young Washington.

Washington's task as military administrator was thankless. Supplies and equipment of all kinds were lacking. Recruiting went slowly; most of the men who were cajoled into enlisting were of poor caliber, skilled in nothing but the art of desertion. As a result he acquired a lasting contempt for short-term militia troops. Indeed, he was a Virginia gentleman to whom all enlisted men were social inferiors. He looked after them, but he punished them sternly when they transgressed. Thus he wrote to Dinwiddie in August 1757:

I send your Honor a copy of the proceedings of a General Court Martial. Two of those condemned, namely, Ignatious Edwards, and Wm. Smith, were hanged on thursday last. . . . Your honor will, I hope excuse my hanging instead of shooting them. It conveyed much terror to others; and it was for example sake, we did it. They were proper objects to suffer: Edwards had deserted twice before, and Smith was accounted one of the greatest villians upon the continent. Those who were intended to be whipped, have received their punishment accordingly; and I should be glad to know what your Honor wou'd choose to have done with the rest?

"The rest" were subsequently pardoned; Washington had been keeping them "in a dark room, closely ironed."

Often he could get no explicit instructions. "My orders," he complained in December 1756, "are dark, doubtful, and uncertain; *to-day approved, to-morrow condemned.*" His whole position was ambiguous and anomalous, giving him the semblance of power but not much actual authority. He and his force in 1754 received less pay than troops from other colonies. Though a colonel, he was outranked by every captain who happened to hold a royal (or regular) commission instead of a militia one. A Captain Mackay who brought a company from North Carolina in 1754 would not acknowledge Colonel Washington as his chief; nor, a few months later, would a Captain Dagworthy whose royal commission was only a memory since he had retired and sold his pension rights. And Washington must have known that British regular officers as a group were disdainful of the provincials (one of them referred to Virginia militia officers as "Jockeys," and another remarked privately that "a planter is not to be taken from the plough and made an officer in a day").

All this understandably irritated Washington. The striking feature is that it did more; it rankled with him, it drove him to the pitch of fury. Granted that he was honest and competent, we must feel that he insisted on his own virtues too often in his letters to Dinwiddie and others. One clue is provided by the fact that, back in 1753, he *volunteered* to bear Dinwiddie's ultimatum to the French. If that was the act of a brave and patriotic Virginian, it was also the act of an extremely ambitious young man. His subsequent acts and correspondence reveal that he was not a wild romantic. Reputation, though sought in the cannon's mouth, was not for him a bubble but a solid matter of recognition and reward. He had, so to speak, speculated on "the Art Military." To be a planter was something; he glimpsed another and more dazzling possibility – the "honor" and "preferment" that came from the Crown.

The word "preferment," as applied to his own career, occurs more than once in Washington's letters of this period. Even in Virginia it was vital to know the right people; in the larger world everything might depend upon reinforcing merit with patronage. Daniel Parke, a well-connected Virginian who served as a volunteer with the Duke of Marlborough, was rewarded by Queen Anne with one thousand guineas and her miniature portrait set in diamonds, when he brought her the news of the victory of Blenheim in 1704. This was an exceptional piece of luck, especially when followed by Parke's appointment to the governorship of the Leeward Islands. Washington's hopes hardly soared so high. But he knew that as a provincial militia officer he was far down the ladder of preferment. Perhaps he was not even on it at all.

So he longed for a regular commission (after all, his brother Lawrence had held one) to give him an identity, a stake. In 1754 he had been in the world's eye, temporarily – almost a symbolic figure in the vast imperial drama of Britain and France. In 1755, as one of Braddock's inner circle of privileged young gentlemen, he had again stood near the forefront. He had served with distinction afterward. Looking back on his career as a whole, it might appear that the young Virginian advanced in renown without a break. We could, as many biographers have done, lay stress on the words of the minister who in a sermon of 1755, on the disaster at the Monongahela, singled out Colonel Washington as an American hero whom Providence might have marked for great things. But in his own view, at least in pessimistic moments, these were lost years – in every sense, years in the wilderness. His services went unrecognized; his luck was out. Braddock was killed; Braddock's successors seemed unimpressed by Washington's talents. How, then, could he make his point? If he failed, it was not for want of trying. When Lord Loudoun became commander in chief in North America, Washington wrote (January 1757):

> Altho' I had not the honor to be known to your Lordship, your Lordship's name was familiar to my ear, on account of the important services performed to his Majesty in other parts of the world. Do not think, my Lord, that I am going to flatter; notwithstanding I have exalted sentiments of your Lordship's character and respect your rank, it is not my intention to adulate. My nature is open and honest and free from guile! . . . With regard to myself, I cannot forbear adding, that had his Excellency General Braddock survived his unfortunate defeat, I

should have met with preferment agreeable to my wishes. I had his promise to that purpose, and I believe that gentleman was too sincere and generous to make unmeaning offers.

By the spring of 1758 he said he had "laid aside all hopes of preferment in the Military line." Nevertheless, he sent two slightly unctuous letters to British regular officers of his acquaintance, asking them to recommend him to General Forbes "as one who would gladly be distinguished . . . from the *common run* of provincial officers." And in June 1758 he welcomed the arrival of Dinwiddie's successor, Lieutenant Governor Fauquier, with a similar assortment of overdone flattery and modesty.

In other words, he did everything feasible to win preferment (he rode all the way to Boston in 1756, to establish with the commander in chief his precedence over Captain Dagworthy) – everything, that is, short of dishonor. There is something unlikable about the George Washington of 1753-1758. He seems a trifle raw and strident, too much on his dignity, too ready to complain, too nakedly concerned with promotion. Yet he had real grievances; he was efficient and resolute. His fault lay in saying so too frequently to other people, and in nearly developing a persecution complex as his hopes faded after a promising, almost sensational early start. "I have long been convinced," he reiterated to Dinwiddie in October 1757, "that my actions and their motives have been maliciously aggravated." He had yet to learn the wisdom of patience; or rather, he was learning it in a painful school.

Otherwise, his shortcomings were more than balanced by his good qualities. His outlook was rather narrowly Virginian. He did not conceive of the war as a whole; when Forbes chose the Raystown route in 1758, Washington's hostility persisted close to the point of insubordination. He was sure that Forbes was the victim of a Pennsylvania "artifice," by which the rival colony would get itself a road into the back country and so steal the trade of the Ohio frontier. It did not seem to occur to him that his own attitude might be construed as a Virginia "artifice." But at any rate he *was* loyal to Virginia. What he wanted, ideally, was a regular commission to defend Virginia. If he had wanted a royal commission on any terms, he could have purchased one, as young Bryan Fairfax did.

With the longing for preferment went the thirst for "honor." Sometimes Washington defined this so as to make it almost synonymous with preferment. It also meant to him, however, the "friendly regard of my acquaintances" (with Sally Fairfax perhaps high on the list). All through his adult life Washington was to be closely concerned with his reputation. In part this was simply an aspect of his canniness – a matter of taking care that there was a written record of everything that was done to him as well as by him. Beyond this, though, Washington needed the solace of public approval. He was determined to do what was right, and he hoped that his rectitude would be acknowledged even if his actions turned out badly. In the last resort, honor (and honor within his own colony) mattered more than preferment. Colonel Washington was a man on the make, but he was fundamentally a decent man. His military ambitions, though considerable in their way, had never been inordinate. And so he was able to tuck them away in a corner of his mind. How deeply buried they were we cannot tell. We know that in 1759, when he was embellishing Mount Vernon, he ordered six portrait busts from London. They were of Alexander the Great, Julius Caesar, Charles XII of Sweden, Frederick II of Prussia, Prince Eugene and "the Duke of Marlborh" – all military heroes. His agent was unable to supply them, but Washington did not accept the busts of poets and philosophers that were proffered instead.

At a time of despondency Colonel Fairfax had consoled him with the observation that "having Caesar's Commentaries and perhaps Quintus Curtious [the author of a life of Alexander] You have therein read of greater Fatigues, Murmurings, Mutinys and Defections, than will probably come to your Share, tho if any of these casualtys should interrupt your Quiet I doubt not but You would bear them with equal Magnanimity those Heroes remarkably did."

If, on retiring, Washington was still in need of consolation, he could reflect that Caesar was murdered and that Alexander, while a king at nineteen, was dead at thirty-two. General Wolfe, one of his own contemporaries, had a brilliant career, but he too died at thirty-two in the capture of Quebec. Of Washington's associates none had far outstripped him, and some had disgraced themselves. Others were dead – his old companion Christopher Gist, for example, who had succumbed to smallpox. Thanks to his illness in Barbados, Washington was at least immune to that particular scourge.

THE RETIRED PLANTER

He had more tangible grounds for content. The Fairfaxes were still his friends. He had valuable properties, and the hope of adding to them when the French troubles were over. Above all, he was ending his bachelor days. His bride was an amiable, prosperous young widow,

Martha Dandridge Custis, whose first husband was descended from the Daniel Parke who had borne the Blenheim dispatches to Queen Anne. Martha was a few months older than George and had two children by her first marriage. When he first met her, or how their courtship developed, is uncertain. A love letter he is supposed to have sent her in the summer of 1758 appears to be a forgery. There is some evidence to suggest that at about the time of the betrothal, George was still emotionally disturbed by Sally Fairfax; a letter to her may be interpreted as a confession of love. It is doubtful whether George and Martha's was a love match as a romantic novelist might understand the term. For both it was a prudent engagement. Among other things, Martha gained a manager for her holdings and George married a fortune. But there is no reason to suppose that it was simply a marriage of convenience, or that George turned to Martha as a desperate substitute for Sally. No one whose opinion has survived ever suggested that their marriage was inharmonious or inappropriate; and it is likely that any sign of strain between them, at any stage in their long connection, would have provoked a good deal of comment.

George was married in January 1759, and in September he wrote to a kinsman in London:

> I am now I believe fixed at this Seat with an agreeable Consort
> for Life and hope to find more happiness in retirement than I
> ever experienc'd amidst a wide and bustling World.

True, in the same letter he regrets that he cannot visit London despite the "longing desire, which for many years I have had" because "I am now tied by the Leg and must set Inclination aside." But there are no other indications that he found life with Martha irksome. The remarkable thing is that he adapted himself so rapidly to an existence in such sharp contrast with the one he had led in places like Fort Cumberland.

One explanation must be that Washington had in fact, as he claimed, wearied of soldiering and relinquished his expectations of military preferment. There remained the other road to distinction, a less thrilling but a steadier one — that of the Virginia landowner. A second explanation is that Washington was extremely busy. There was much work to be done on the Mount Vernon farms, which were in poor condition through his absence. The house had to be furnished on an adequate scale; crowded invoices were sent to London, covering everything from "1 Tester Bedstead 7½ feet pitch" to "the newest, and most approv'd Treatise of Agriculture," from "40 Yds. Of coarse Jeans or fustian, for Summer Frocks for Negroe Servts." to "6 little books for Childn begg. to Read." The children beginning to read were George's stepchildren, John Parke (Jackie) and Martha Parke (Patsy) Custis. He also ordered toys and trinkets for them. Indeed, he was to take endless trouble with them and with all the other children who came within his circle. Cynics might say that Jackie and Patsy imposed a very pleasant burden upon him, since their estate and their mother's brought him considerable wealth. But that seems a harsh judgment, from what else we know of him.

It may sound absurd to use the word patriarch in connection with an active young man of twenty-seven. There was, however, something patriarchal in his way of life. He presided over a domain at Mount Vernon that was in effect a little village. By degrees Mount Vernon became the headquarters of the Washington clan. George was the most successful of all the brothers and sisters, who looked to him for advice and succor. When he was not dealing with the affairs of his own family, or considering the appeals of hard-up acquaintances, Washington had to manage the Custis properties. As a burgess he had to attend sessions at Williamsburg, and to keep his electors content. Not long after his marriage he joined the bench as a county magistrate. Then, following in his father's footsteps, he became a vestryman of Truro Parish (and later a churchwarden). In 1766 he filled a vacant place as a trustee of Alexandria. Moreover, he was still a keen speculator who bought land whenever the opportunity arose. He persisted, with ultimate success, in his claim to fifteen thousand acres of the bounty land that had been promised to the volunteers of 1754. He joined in land ventures like the Dismal Swamp Company (in southern Virginia) and the Mississippi Company (which proposed to develop a tract on the Mississippi River). Still young in years, he was relatively old in responsibility.

By the time he was forty, Colonel Washington was a substantial figure in Virginia, though not yet among the small circle of enormously powerful men. Perhaps he still remembered his military years with a tinge of regret and disappointment. Perhaps there is some significance to the fact that when he posed for his portrait to Charles Willson Peale in 1772, he dressed himself in the uniform of a Virginia colonel of militia. But it seems more likely that he chose this uniform because he was fond of fine clothes and knew that he looked particularly distinguished in military raiment. The face that gazes at us from that portrait is of a man in his prime who is at peace with the world. It is the face of a man who leads a full and active life and is thereby preserved from boredom or smugness, who is not gnawed by envy or driven on by some private demon of aggressive ambition, or kept awake at night by a load of debt, the threat of betrayal, the torment of a bad conscience. It is the face of a man who has a place in the community, near the head of things — and, one would guess, of a family man.

Since this is very much what Washington was, we can conclude that it was an accurate portrait. He had no children of his own; however he was a family man as far as Martha's children were concerned. While he did not fret over them with as much nervous solicitude as Martha, he evidently shared her protective love for her sickly daughter and her charming but somewhat wayward son. Their anxiety over Patsy mounted as the girl became increasingly subject to "convulsions," or epileptic fits; and to their grief she died in 1773, when she was only seventeen. However, Jackie was married a few months later, to pretty Nelly Calvert of Maryland. His stepfather-guardian complained at the suddenness of the match — the impatient Jackie could not wait to finish college — but accepted the situation with indulgent good humor. Before long Jackie had two children to engage the grandfatherly affections of Colonel Washington. He was uncle or guardian to a whole brood of other children.

One dearly wishes that we had another, earlier portrait to set beside Peale's.[7] If we could see Washington in, say, 1757, we should get a glimpse of an individual who was far less mature. As he confronts us in 1772, we can understand why adjectives such as "sagacious" were so often applied to him. He seems poised, almost benign — the master of himself and his surroundings. In 1757, by contrast, he might have appeared able but a trifle on edge. We can almost imagine him scowling a little and adopting a belligerent stance, like those anonymous, pathetic young heroes, a century later, in daguerreotypes of the Civil War.

In the intervening years George Washington, as we can clearly gather from his correspondence, grew in moral stature. This is not to say that he underwent any sudden conversion. The road back to Mount Vernon was not for him the road to Damascus. Ignatius Loyola was a warrior until he sickened of bloodshed while convalescing at Pamplona; so was Francesco Bernardone until he turned back in the middle of an expedition, to start existence afresh as Francis of Assisi. Not so George Washington. There was no moment of revelation. It is true that he was a sound Episcopalian, but his religion, though no doubt perfectly

---

[7] There is in fact a miniature portrait, attributed to OJ. S. Copley, which used to be accepted as a likeness of Washington done in 1757. This now seems most unlikely; and in any case, the portrait is too mild and innocuous to suggest the character of its subject, whoever he may be.

sincere, was a social performance, quite lacking in angels or visions – except for those that Parson Weems contrived for him. He was a Christian as a Virginia planter understood the term. He seems never to have taken communion; he stood to pray, instead of kneeling; and he did not invariably go to church on Sundays. Perhaps illness had an effect upon him, as it had – more dramatically – upon Loyola and Saint Francis. He was dangerously sick in the winter of 1757-1758, and again in 1761, when he wrote that "I once thought the grim King would certainly master my utmost efforts and that I must sink in spite of a noble struggle." The prospect of death does concentrate a man's mind.

Yet there is not very much to be got out of the attempt to visualize Washington as a warrior saint. The most we can say (and it is a good deal) is that, like Loyola or Saint Francis, he showed a capacity for growth; his character improved, if not to the point of sanctity. Thus a biographer investigating Washington's career up to 1759 could maintain that Washington was tight, even stingy, where money was involved. For instance, when Washington was forced to hand Van Braam over to the French as a hostage at Fort Necessity, he sold Van Braam a dress uniform which he might otherwise have found a nuisance to carry away with him. It was not a shameful transaction, but it was a brisk one. After his retirement, however, Washington lent money with an almost reckless generosity, when he often had no guarantee of getting it back. Sometimes he gave his support privately and unasked. Worldly success spoils many people; it suited Washington.

So, as we observe him in the Peale portrait, the Washington of the early 1770s was a contented, upright man. He was a man of his time and place. A quarter of a century later he was to provide magnanimously in his will that his slaves be set free after Martha's death. But in 1766 slavery for Washington was hardly a moral issue. He did only what he and his neighbors would have thought proper when, in that year, he sent a "Rogue and Runaway" Negro slave named Tom to be sold in the West Indies, instructing the schooner captain to keep Tom "handcuffed till you get to Sea or in the Bay," and to bring back out of the purchase money molasses, rum, limes, tamarinds and other goods. This seems to have been the only instance, however, of such a deal on Washington's part, and by contemporary standards he appears to have been a decent master. And, too, a planter of unusual intelligence and diligence. His books were not always balanced with the precision that a latter-day chartered accountant might enjoin. But they compared favorably with those of his neighbors. He strove to improve his land and its harvest, recognizing that tobacco brought a poor yield, that fertilizer was a necessity, that wheat and flour-milling, fish from the Potomac and cloth woven at home were all possible ways of making the Mount Vernon estates show a profit. He kept a careful eye – and no doubt a gratified eye, since they prospered – on the Custis lands along the York River. When he was not supervising his plantations or occupied with other duties, he diverted himself with dances, card games and riding to hounds. He also entertained on a liberal scale. In the seven years up to 1775 about two thousand guests visited Mount Vernon, most of whom stayed to dinner and many of whom remained overnight. Apart from his attendances at Williamsburg, business or pleasure took him to Annapolis, Fredericksburg, the Dismal Swamp and elsewhere. In 1770 he made a long trip to the frontier, past Fort Pitt and down the Ohio by canoe, to seek out possible land claims. He planned another western trip for 1775.

Yet in the early summer of 1775, instead of working out the details of a western journey, he was heading northward to Boston. George Washington, Esquire, was now General Washington; the loyal Virginia gentleman was a rebel – indeed, the military leader not merely of Virginia but of all the thirteen American colonies from Georgia to Massachusetts.

THE MODEST PATRIOT

There is not room enough here to analyze this staggering development in any detail. Briefly, we can see that there were three main causes of colonial intransigence. The first was the removal (thanks to the victorious war of 1756-1763) of the French threat. By the peace of 1763 France gave up all her possessions in North America. Once her power was ended, so in great measure was colonial dependence upon the mother country. The second cause, which followed logically from the first, was the attempt of Britain to reorganize her colonial empire. Some degree of reorganization was inevitable, since Britain had conquered the Canadian provinces. To colonials it also appeared that Britain had inherited French conceptions of empire in the back country between the Alleghenies and the Mississippi, by reserving the area for Indians and fur traders. Such seems to be the motive behind the Proclamation of 1763, which forbade white settlement beyond the Allegheny watershed, while the Quebec Act of 1774 designated as Canadian territory all land north of the Ohio River. In the intervening years the mother country had tried to create a more systematic imperial structure, embracing the older as well as the newly won dominions. The seaboard colonies were now required to pay their share of the costs of empire, through taxes that would also define more sharply the mercantilist pattern, according to which the colonies supplied raw materials to Britain and provided a market for Britain's manufactures. The proposed taxes were not burdensome in themselves; the colonies as a whole were prosperous and under lighter fiscal burdens than the mother country.

What irked the American colonies – and here we come to the third cause – was the assumption that they were not parts of Britain but possessions of Britain. In actuality they were mature, or nearly so, in modes of life and in habits of self-government. But the mother country regarded them as infants, to be indulged when they behaved obediently and spanked when they were naughty. It was not at heart a question of tyranny, whatever patriotic orators said, but of minor grievances that took on the semblance of major ones because the parent was muddled and obstinate and patronizing, while the offspring were on an age to want their own way. "Is it the interest of a man to be a boy all his life?" Tom Paine put the question in his pamphlet *Common Sense,* in 1776; and for more than ten years, with varying answers, others had been asking themselves the same question.

Certain broad attitudes were common to all the colonies, or to the equivalent groups within them. The merchant of Boston could understand the merchant of Philadelphia. The Southern planter took rank with the well-established proprietor of New York; indeed, George Washington may have cast a matrimonial eye at the daughter of one of them when he passed through New York in 1756. Lawyers everywhere spoke the same language, and so did the less articulate settlers along the enormous colonial frontier. Within each colony were special sources of dissatisfaction. Tidewater Virginia was preoccupied with an alarmingly unstable economy. Even a carefully run plantation such as Mount Vernon brought its owner little profit (though Washington augmented his farm income by constructing a flour mill and exporting barrels of fish caught in the Potomac). Tobacco prices were low, and the crop impoverished the soil. Currency was scarce, and since Virginia bought more than it sold, the colony's planters – Washington among them – fell in debt to British merchants who, it was alleged, often cheated their helpless victims. Washington himself began to grow wheat instead of tobacco at Mount Vernon, to halt the drain on his resources. The alert speculator could still look to the west; but the British proclamations threatened to hinder him, and the British speculators began to compete with him through the Walpole Grant. The Ohio Company's claims were rejected by the home government in favor of some speculators from Pennsylvania.

The picture should not be painted too black. For one thing, the mother country was not entirely to blame for the swing in Virginia's fortunes, and until the eve of conflict she was not held wholly responsible. Again, though her land policy was irritating, it did not strangle Virginia enterprise; Washington was able to patent twenty-four thousand acres of land in the Ohio and Kanawha valleys, apart from the twelve thousand acres he owned in the settled areas. Nor should we make too much of the loss of prestige the British are supposed to have suffered as a result of Braddock's defeat. Even if Washington and his fellow Virginians focused upon events in their own colony, they must have been aware of the British feats of arms at Louisbourg and Quebec. They knew that after 1763 a subject of King George III was a member of the strongest nation in the world. When the Virginian spoke of "my country," he meant Britain *and* its fifth dominion, Virginia, in one splendid entity. If he was in debt to tradesmen for wine or elegant clothes or household articles, so was many another English gentleman nearer London.

But pride wore a double aspect. "Our government," said William Byrd in 1735, "is so happily constituted that a Governor must first outwit us before he can oppress us, and if he ever squeeze money out of us he must first take care to deserve it." Thirty years later, when Britain passed the Stamp Act, Americans did not agree that the proposed revenue was deserved. They took their stand as liberty-loving Britons; their eloquence arose naturally out of their heritage and out of their own circumstances. Some were more fluent than others: in Virginia, the erudite young Thomas Jefferson, the vehement Patrick Henry or the more seasoned George Mason found the words that struck a response. But the debate, by turns curiously lofty and curiously practical, widened throughout the colonies. The word "speculation" held its ancient meaning, even for the solid planter Colonel Washington; the Stamp Act, he wrote in 1765, "engrosses the conversation of the *speculative* part of the Colonists" (my italics).

In that year, neither Washington nor any other colonist was contemplating disunion. The American case found support at home in England; the Stamp Act was repealed; and Washington in correspondence with his merchants could still say, as an Englishman to Englishmen, that all "who were instrumental in procuring the repeal are entitled to the thanks of every British subject and have mine cordially." However, in the same letter he speaks of the ominous consequences of nonrepeal; and this hard edge became apparent again in his letters in another three or four years. The Stamp Act had been followed by other taxation by the mother country in the shape of the Townshend Acts. Washington was sufficiently aroused to play a leading part among Virginians in 1769-1770 in agreeing not to import taxable goods from Britain. "Addresses to the throne and remonstrances to Parliament we have already, it is said, proved the efficacy of," he told his friend and neighbor George Mason of Gunston Hall; "how far their attention to our rights and privileges is to be awakened or alarmed by starving their trade and manufactures, remains to be tried." He also wrote firmly to Mason that if need be, as a "last resource," Americans should be prepared to take up arms to defend their ancestral liberties "from the inroads of our lordly Masters . . . in Great Britain." Few anticipated that the dispute would be put to the test of overt violence. Once more the home government yielded to pressure. All the Townshend duties were repealed, except that on tea imported by the colonies. Perhaps the trouble would all blow over. Prominent men such as Washington had, after all, plenty of private business to attend to. Arguments lost their savor through repetition.

But at the end of 1773 a well-drilled party of radicals in Boston staged the celebrated Tea Party, throwing some cargoes of tea into the harbor rather than pay duty upon it. Conscious or not of the emblematic meaning, the Bostonians concerned disguised themselves as Indians — the true natives of the American continent. Their action and the wanton destruction it accomplished were not universally endorsed in the colonies. However, the retaliatory, coercive legislation enacted by Parliament against Massachusetts, which was viewed as the ringleader among the colonies, brought the rest to her support.

In Virginia, Washington was again one of the principal agents in the gathering crisis. He was not one of the extremists ("a modest man, but sensible and speaks little – in action cool, like a Bishop at his prayers," he was described in 1774), but took the middle ground between fiery radicals such as Patrick Henry and worried conservatives such as Attorney General John Randolph. Thus, though he defended the experiment of "non-importantation," he was opposed to the further scheme of "non-exportation," on the grounds that Virginians could not pay their due debts to British creditors unless they were allowed to continue to export their products.

Yet once he made his mind up, he did not conceal his views. And while he was not himself an articulate controversialist he painstakingly absorbed the arguments of those who were: George Mason, for example, whose lucid propositions he put forward as "resolves" at a Fairfax County meeting in July 1774. As a burgess of long standing, he moved forward step by step with his fellows in the Virginia House of Assembly toward something like open revolt.

Some dropped behind, horrified by the atmosphere of defiance; Randolph was not the only wealthy Virginian with misgivings. Why, even, as another wealthy Virginian, should he not have become a loyalist and left the colony, as Randolph did? After all, Washington's father and two half brothers were all educated in England. His near neighbors and close friends the Fairfaxes were English in sentiment. Bryan Fairfax, the brother of Colonel George William Fairfax (Sally's husband), wrote to him to plead for reconciliation with the mother country. Why was he so unimpressed by Bryan's arguments?

The answer seems evident enough; or it did to Washington. Not only did his own nature impel him to resistance; "the voice of mankind is with me." By *mankind* he no doubt meant Virginia. He was a Virginian by birth, upbringing, instinct and – not least – by property. Here were his lands; here he belonged. If his fellows felt as he did, that was all that he needed, being a straightforward man, by way of reassurance.

There are tantalizing possibilities to consider in the story. What if his relations with Dinwiddie had remained sweeter? Or if Braddock had not died in the wilderness battle near Duquesne but had beaten the French, and, in the generous glow of victory, had recommended his Virginia aide to royal patronage? What if, in short, Washington had been awarded his precious royal commission? The war against the French had lasted several more years – long enough for him to fight on many fields outside Virginia, long enough to forge new ties and weaken old ones. It is an intriguing thought.

But the minute accidents of history combined otherwise, Colonel Washington of Mount Vernon, attending the Virginia Provincial Convention at Williamsburg in August 1774, was drawn further into the conflict. His opinions were formed in what was, in a sense, a borrowed vocabulary (he listened a great deal to talk about "natural right," "law and the constitution" and so on) but in what was – more importantly – a *shared* vocabulary. That autumn he was elected as one of seven Virginia delegates to a meeting of all the thirteen colonies, the First Continental Congress in Philadelphia.

Thomas Jefferson was too ill to be nominated; and George Mason, not being a burgess, was excluded. Even so, the choice of Washington – apparently with a substantial vote – shows that in the esteem of his peers he was now among the most important Virginians who sympathized with the colonies rather than with the Crown. He could dine with the royal governor without being suspected of temporizing. His rise had been unobtrusive, yet unmistakable. Patrick Henry, another of the seven delegates, was more likely to say the magnificent thing; Washington could be counted upon to do the right thing, according to decency and common sense.

At Philadelphia, sure enough, he heard Patrick Henry declare in moving tones, "I am not a Virginian, but an American" – a novel notion, belonging at present more to rhetoric than reality. Here, too, news reached the Congress that British troops had occupied Boston and were fortifying it – a monstrous act, they all felt. Agreement was harder to reach on other elements in the situation. Indignation was all very well; what precise forms should it take? The delegates, John Adams wrote home to his wife, were fifty strangers, "not acquainted with each other's language, ideas, views, designs. They are, therefore, jealous of each other – fearful, timid, skittish." There was a good deal of oratory and verbal maneuver. Each delegate took his own emotional temperature, so to speak, and that of all the others. Washington was a rather silent participant, though not an unsociable one. In a situation where everyone tended to talk too much, his reserve was probably an asset.

Nor was the occasion futile in other ways. Agreement was reached on various peaceful measures of protest and opposition, and the Congress adjourned until the spring of 1775. Washington was again chosen as a Virginia delegate. When he arrived back in Philadelphia from Mount Vernon in May 1775, to attend the Second Continental Congress, he wore uniform – the only uniform in the gathering, as it chanced. On the way, he reviewed a number of volunteer companies; and his companions in Philadelphia could report similar signs of popular excitement in the districts they had traveled through. Indeed, temperatures were rising everywhere. In April, at Lexington and Concord, there had been a prolonged skirmish between Massachusetts militiamen and British regulars from the Boston garrison, who had been roughly handled in the affair. In May, just after Washington reached Philadelphia, a body of colonials captured Fort Ticonderoga, at the northern end of Lake George – the main route to Canada. At about the same time, in his own Virginia, the men of Patrick Henry's Hanover County were openly challenging the governor's authority.

No one could predict the outcome of so much unrest. But the colonies had banded together. The bolder spirits represented in the Continental Congress were ready to answer force with force. They needed an army and the army needed a commander. On June 15, 1775, it was resolved that "a General be appointed to command all the continental forces raised for the defence of American liberty." The day before, in Congress, the influential John Adams of Massachusetts, supported by his persuasive colleague and namesake Samuel Adams, had put forward the name of Colonel Washington. The Virginian, probably taken by surprise and certainly confused by the sudden eulogy, slipped out of the room. He stayed away on the fifteenth, when his name was put in formal nomination by a Maryland delegate and when as a result "George Washington Esq. was unanimously elected."

CHAPTER THREE
GENERAL WASHINGTON

Let us appear nor rash nor diffident:
Immoderate valour swells into a fault,
And fear, admitted into public councils,
Betrays like treason. Let us shun them both.

ADDISON'S *Cato*, Act II, Scene I

COMMAND AND CRISIS: 1775-1776

Posterity accepts George Washington as the only conceivable choice for the post of commander in chief. But why did the delegates at Philadelphia pick him out? Only in part for military reasons. Several other men in the colonies had seen as much service and could claim to have acquitted themselves as satisfactorily. One or two – notably Charles Lee and Horatio Gates, former English regular officers who now upheld the American cause – had had considerably more experience of soldiering. And Artemas Ward of Massachusetts was already in the field, directing the New England militia around Boston.

Yet Washington was chosen, unanimously. He would probably have been passed over if he had not himself been a delegate, and become known and trusted. As it was, he did not contribute much in set discussion. But he made an excellent impression, in committee and at private dinner tables, as a man of sense and sincerity. Though Samuel Curwen, who met Washington at Philadelphia in May 1775, was a staunch loyalist who soon after departed for England, he admitted that the Virginia colonel was "a fine figure and of a most easy and agreeable address." The members of Congress confirmed Curwen's opinion: "an easy, soldierlike air," one of them noted, with the added comment that Washington had "a very young look." At forty-three he was exactly the right age to combine vigor with "sound information."

Moreover, Washington was a wealthy man, if not quite as rich as rumor had it (or he himself perhaps believed). The New York delegates had been instructed beforehand:

> On a General in America, fortune also should bestow her gifts, that he may rather communicate lustre to his dignities than receive it, and that his country in his property, his kindred, and connexions, may have sure pledges that he will faithfully perform the duties of his high office, and readily lay down his power when the general weal shall require it.

No one could have better fitted this description. Washington revealed himself as an aristocrat with radical leanings. At any rate, unlike some of the prominent citizens at Philadelphia, he was prepared to commit himself and his estates on the side of the colonies. His military apparel proclaimed the fact; his demeanor and his reputation preserved him from the charge of flamboyance. The first signs of the myth-making process appeared. A rumor got about in 1775 that in the previous year Colonel Washington had offered to raise and lead to Boston a regiment of a thousand Virginians, paying for them out of his own pocket. The rumor seems to be entirely without foundation, though biographers have often repeated it as true. But it shows how eagerly the men at Philadelphia cast about for evidences of greatness, for the lineaments of the altogether exceptional man. In Sam Adams and others Congress had patriots who could rouse a rabble; its imperative need was for someone who could discipline and lead a rabble, who could both look and behave like a commander on the European model and yet be a true American.

There was one other important consideration. So far, the clash had been confined to New England. If the other colonies were to join in fully, the command of the proposed Continental army would have to be given – as John and Samuel Adams realized – to a soldier from outside New England. With Massachusetts, Virginia held preeminence in colonial power. As a Virginian, George Washington was therefore all the more eligible. In the parlance of more recent American history, he was the "available" candidate, and his subordinate major generals were appointed with due regard for the political and other factors involved: Artemas Ward to appease Massachusetts; the much-traveled Charles Lee for his military sophistication; Philip Schuyler (another delegate, a rich man and a seasoned military officer) to satisfy New York; and Israel Putnam as a favorite son and folk hero of Connecticut. Horatio Gates, British by birth and a Virginian by adoption, was appointed adjutant general. As their juniors, several brigadier generals were chosen from similarly mixed motives.

Perhaps it is misleading to use the word "candidate" in relation to Washington. He had not thrust himself forward; he was undoubtedly sincere in assuring Congress that he did "not think myself equal to the command," and there is a story that he even confided to Patrick Henry, with tears in his eyes, that "from the day I enter upon the command of the American armies, I date my fall, and the ruin of my reputation." The story may not be authentic, but there is no doubt that Washington still retained a high sense of his own good name. Though he protested in many a letter that he did not mind criticism, and though he had to withstand a great deal of it, to the end of his days he never learned to accept it as one of the inevitable trials of public office. He kept his anger within bounds; in contrast to many of his contemporaries he excluded dueling from his code of honor. But he cared intensely, not because he was conceited but because he was proud. He detested shabby behavior in others, and could not bear that they should attribute petty instincts to him. Once before, as a gentleman volunteer under Braddock, he had shown his disinterestedness by serving without pay and without formal rank. He now repeated the gesture on a grander scale, by informing Congress that he required no salary; he would accept only his expenses (Congress had decided on an allowance of five hundred dollars a month for the commander in chief's pay and expenses).

If almost overwhelmed by the responsibility that had been put upon him, he would have been inhuman not to be profoundly gratified by the compliment it implied. He had never allowed his former military disappointments to rankle. But whatever the regrets he had once nourished, they were canceled at a stroke. A long time ago the young Washington had written to Sally Fairfax that he would dearly like to play Juba to her Marcia, in Addisons' *Cato*. Marcia was Cato's daughter, and Juba was a Numidian princeling, one of Cato's supporters. That theatrical dream belonged to the buried past; Sally Fairfax had sailed for England with her husband in 1773, and was never to return to America. The same play, though, was performed at Washington's headquarters, Valley Forge, in May 1778; and possibly, though he was not given to such fancies, the thought might have occurred to General Washington that in his image the young half-alien Juba had been recast as the full Roman and acknowledged leader, Cato. When he took over command of the patriot army outside Boston, the date – July 3, 1775 – was another reminder of the distance he had traveled in his career. It was the twenty-first anniversary of his surrender to the French at Fort Necessity. The youthful colonel had been trapped by a superior force; the mature man was himself the besieger, at the head of not far short of fifteen thousand militia. Inside Boston was less than half that number of British troops, who a fortnight earlier had lost a thousand men in their expensive victory at Breed's Hill. Their commander, General Gage, had led Braddock's ill-fated advance guard twenty years before, when Washington was a junior aide-de-camp.

At the time, however, such consolations were dwarfed by a mass of problems. There was the wrench of leaving Martha and his cherished Virginia estates. There were all the worries of command. Many of the New Englanders were suspicious of Washington, and he was suspicious of many of them – as he revealed in some indiscreet correspondence. He complained that "Order, Regularity and Discipline" were lacking. So, as a concrete result of what he regarded as Yankee slovenliness and dishonesty, were supplies of tents, blankets, uniforms, medicine, food, ammunition and powder. There was virtually no staff, or artillery. Until Congress made provision, there was no proper pay chest. Congress had determined to raise a Continental army; would all the states respond by furnishing the quotas asked for? The answer to this particular question was more no than yes, and was to remain thus throughout the war years.

What was to be done, actively, with the forces available? Neither Congress nor Washington could develop far-reaching plans. As at Fort Necessity, the opposing troops were not formally at war. The Americans spoke of General Gage's British army in Boston as the "ministerial" troops – maintaining the argument that the colonies were still loyal to

King George, and that they were merely standing up for their rights as free subjects of His Majesty. In the closing months of 1775 only an extremist minority favored complete independence. The majority of Americans hoped for an "accommodation" with the mother country, though its shape was hard to envisage. In the meantime, a bold front was necessary; but what could be done? Congress had made tentative overtures to the Canadian provinces; Washington took the step of sending an expedition under Colonel Benedict Arnold to seize Quebec and clinch the matter. With equal boldness he more than once proposed an assault on Boston. But Arnold's invasion was a gallant failure, and the council of war at Washington's headquarters voted down the suggested assault.

It has been said that Washington deferred too readily to his subordinates. If so, his hesitations are understandable in view of "the limited and contracted knowledge, which any of us have in military matters." Even Charles Lee, despite his conversational flow, had had no practical experience in maneuvering large formations. Washington's service had been confined to frontier warfare, in a relatively junior capacity. He had no firsthand acquaintance with cavalry tactics or the use of massed artillery, not to mention the handling of a large composite force. He could not afford to trust his own judgment while so much remained a closed book to him. Moreover, in holding councils of war he was actually conforming to a practice common to all armies and all commanders of the day. Again, he had to be as tactful as possible in dealing with men senior in years who at first were inclined to resent that he had been put over them. This was particularly the case with Artemas Ward. Five years older than Washington, he too had served as a colonel of militia in the French wars and felt that he had so far been more than a match for Gage at Boston. Israel Putnam, who won anecdotal immortality at Bunker Hill ("Don't fire, boys, until you see the whites of their eyes"), was fourteen years older than Washington and had led an extraordinarily varied and adventurous life. Such men had to be handled with care by a newcomer from another colony – a slaveholder, moreover, and therefore doubly suspect to the New England conscience. Patriots from Connecticut or New Hampshire or Massachusetts did not wish to be ordered about by Southern nabobs. It was just as well in other respects that Washington did consult his generals; although he was sometimes criticized for excessive caution, he was in fact inclined to be too impetuous, as in his younger days. Washington hated inactivity. Against his will he had to wait out the winter of 1775-1776.

With the spring of 1776, one theme at least became gradually clearer amid so much perplexity – the theme of American independence. The desire for independence grew by rapid stages, stimulated by proofs that George III, no less than his ministers (Lord North, Lord George Germain, the Earl of Sandwich and others), was bent on crushing the rebellion. "Arms as the last resource decide the contest; the appeal was the choice of the King, and the Continent has accepted the challenge." So declared Tom Paine in his pamphlet *Common Sense,* whose stirring sentiments met with passionate approval among most of the colonists (including General Washington). A few years earlier, Paine's opinions would have sounded like treason and blasphemy. In the early months of 1776 there was still something shocking in the statement that George III, far from being the best of kings, was simply "the royal Brute of Great Britain." But the shock was delicious, except to horrified loyalists – those whom Nicholas Cresswell, an unfortunate young Englishman who had arrived in the colonies in 1774, referred to in his journal as *Sgnik Sdneirf. Sgnik Sdneirf* was a pathetically transparent code reference to "King's friends." Those whom Cresswell angrily described as *Sleber* – "rebels" in reverse – found that Paine had decisively reversed beliefs in which they had long paid lip service.

> Every thing that is right or reasonable pleads for separation. The blood of the slain, the weeping voice of nature cries, 'TIS TIME TO PART. Even the distance at which the Almighty hath placed England and America is a strong and natural proof, that the authority of the one over the other, was never the design of Heaven.

The course of events that made Paine's eloquence yet more persuasive. The American failure at Quebec and withdrawal from Canada were counterbalanced by the failure of a British expedition by sea, led by General Henry Clinton, against Charleston. Most cheering news of all, Boston was recovered from the British in March 1776. Washington could do little there until he acquired an artillery train. The lack was supplied when the able and energetic young Colonel Henry Knox (a Boston bookseller by trade), after a wearisome winter journey, arrived with forty-three cannon and sixteen mortars. Knox had dragged them overland from Fort Ticonderoga, where they had been captured several months previously. Working at great speed, under cover of darkness, Washington's men installed this ordnance behind breastworks on Dorchester Heights, from which it could dominate Boston and most of the harbor. General William Howe (who had superseded Gage as

British commander in chief) thought of attacking the heights but was dissuaded, perhaps by heavy rain – which was apt to render muskets useless – and possibly by the memory of Bunker Hill, whose carnage he had seen at close quarters. Thanks to American enterprise, Boston was no longer a secure base. Outwitted, if not exactly defeated, Howe embarked his army, took on board a thousand dejected loyalists, destroyed what stores he could, and after lingering a few more days in the harbor, set sail eastward – to Washington's surprise – for Halifax, Nova Scotia. "Sir," Washington wrote to John Hancock, the president of Congress:

> It is with the greatest pleasure I inform you that on Sunday last the 17th. Instant, about 9 O'Clock in the forenoon the Ministerial Army evacuated the Town of Boston, and that the Forces of the United colonies are now in actual Possession thereof. I beg leave to congratulate you, Sir, and the Honorable Congress on this happy event, and particularly as it was effected without endangering the Lives and Property of the remaining unhappy Inhabitants.

Congress replied with a vote of thanks and a gold medal; Washington's praises were sung throughout the land.

At midsummer there was thus no British regular force within the thirteen colonies, except for one led by Sir Guy Carleton, who was pushing down from Canada into northern New York. Congress was in good heart – and would have been even more cheerful had it known that the French, while ostensibly neutral, were planning to strike at their old enemy, Britain, by secretly supplying munitions to the colonies. However, loyalists were active in some areas, especially in the South, and it was apparent that a high proportion of Americans were still *Sgnik Sdneirf* –Tories – or, if not outright Tories, were, in Washington's phrase, "still feeding themselves upon the dainty food of reconciliation." The greater reason, then, to encourage the true patriot and apply pressure to the doubting one. By May 1776 Washington had decided where he stood, and a majority in Congress felt as he did. There was to be no more polite equivocation. A "Ministerial Army" was a royal army; indeed, George III was indicted as the chief villain. It was he who was blamed for hiring German mercenary troops – usually, though rather inaccurately, referred to in the mass as Hessians – and for almost every other offense that a fertile American brain could name. A brain as fertile as Thomas Jefferson's could name a great many, as we may see by reading beyond the splendid preamble and on through all the other clauses of the Declaration of Independence that he drafted, with some assistance, for Congress.

His work received final approval (with the abstention of the New York delegates) on July 4, 1776. Henceforth, for the American leaders, at any rate, there was no turning back. Their aim was complete independence. If they failed, they would be ruined men, destined probably for the hangman's noose. They were sustained by the eloquence of Paine, and now of Jefferson. Even prosaic correspondents such as Washington drew inspiration from the air and spoke with a certain grandeur of their fight for liberty. It was, Washington wrote several times, a "noble" cause, a "just" cause, "as I do most religiously believe it to be," in which Providence would surely aid the brave – and provident.

Yet five months later his vocabulary was altered. He had not lost his nerve, but in common with most other Americans he had almost lost his hope. His army was about to disintegrate; he faced humiliation and disaster. "Our only dependence now," he confessed on December 10 to his cousin Lund Washington, "is upon the speedy enlistment of a new army. If this fails, I think the game will be pretty well up." *The game will be . . . up:* that phrase came so horribly pat that he used it in other correspondence. So, too, another phrase: *choice of difficulties.* "You can form no idea," he told his brother John Augustine, on December 18, "of the perplexity of my Situation. No Man, I believe, ever had a greater choice of difficulties and less means to extricate himself from them."

What had happened between July and December is simply told. Howe was outmaneuvered at Boston. But he had been intending in any case to leave Boston and move his headquarters to a more central base of operations. If he had felt strong enough, he would have sailed direct from Boston to attack New York or Philadelphia. As it was, he retired to Halifax to await reinforcements. These were promised shortly, and the first of them arrived at New York on July 12, in a fleet commanded by his elder brother, Admiral Lord Howe. General Howe had already come ashore on Staten Island, on the very day – July 2 – that Congress took the final vote for independence. In the next few weeks shipload after shipload of British, German and loyalist troops (including Clinton's expedition, back from Charleston) landed on Staten Island, until Howe by mid-August had over thirty thousand soldiers, well clad and well armed, at his disposal.

Washington had been in New York since April, in anticipation of the plan ("We expect a very bloody summer of it at New York," he informed John Augustine on May 31), but was powerless to intervene while the disembarkations continued. There seemed an insolent sureness and deliberation about the process. Supreme at sea – the American navy was insignificant by comparison, a scratch force of prowling privateers – the British seemed about to assert their supremacy on land also. They outnumbered Washington by several thousand. A part of his army consisted of militia, enrolled for short terms, in whom he placed little reliance; and the remainder, the "Continental" nucleus, were engaged to serve only until the end of December. There would have been a good case for abandoning New York. In stern military necessity, a logical course might have been to burn the town and its wharves, leaving the British with a charred ruin on their hands. But there was much to be said against such ruthlessness; Congress in any event instructed Washington to defend the place; and so he was committed to a battle on difficult ground, where the advantage decidedly lay with the side that had superior naval strength.

Nevertheless, if we may judge from the tone of his orders of the day, Washington was reasonably confident. Possibly he was too confident, too eager to offer fight after a whole year in command with only the sham-fight victory of Dorchester Heights to show by way of battle honors. Whatever the reason, he did not acquit himself altogether admirably. The first setback occurred in late August, when Howe at last broke the lull by landing with twenty thousand of his best troops on the tip of Long Island. His obvious aim was to move north and cross to Manhattan by the East River. The way was barred by strong American fortifications on Brooklyn Heights, but most of the eight thousand Americans on Long Island (under General Putnam) were grouped on high ground outside the fortifications. By a serious oversight, which Howe discovered, the American left flank was unprotected. Sending two columns against the American right and center, Howe himself therefore led the main British column round to the American left. His other two detachments had some success, in fairly stiff fighting; Howe, more spectacularly, rolled up the American flank, inflicted two thousand casualties (half of them in prisoners, including Major General John Sullivan of New Hampshire) and had the enemy almost at his mercy, pinned against the East River. Washington must take some of the blame for the faulty American dispositions. He was further in error when he reinforced the American lines at Brooklyn, instead of withdrawing the survivors at the first opportunity.

Fortunately for him, General Howe did not press the assault. Washington quickly recovered, and redeemed himself by evacuating the Brooklyn lines under cover of darkness and a storm that held off Admiral

Howe's ships. His army was now on Manhattan, where it might still be trapped. After some hesitation Washington decided to abandon New York City. By the middle of September his tattered regiments were manning a line across upper Manhattan at Harlem Heights, and Howe was ensconced in New York. It was a cat-and-mouse game; but if Washington was a rather bewildered mouse, Howe proved to be a somnolent cat. Each time the cat stirred itself, the mouse scrambled belatedly away – north from Manhattan to White Plains, and then to North Castle. In the tangled operations that followed, Washington left part of his force with Charles Lee, crossed to New Jersey, and watched in helpless despair while the British captured three thousand patriots whom he had left to hold Fort Washington, at the northern end of Manhattan. There was no course open to Washington, in the gloom of mid-November, but ignominious retreat, pursued southward through New Jersey by one of Howe's field commanders, Lord Cornwallis, and still separated from Charles Lee. The only bright feature was that the American forces led by Schuyler, Horatio Gates and Benedict Arnold were intact and had discouraged Carleton from attempting a campaign down the Champlain-Hudson route toward New York. Elsewhere, there was every reason for depression. True, Charles Lee managed to bring his detachment back to New Jersey, and Washington was able to send for twelve hundred men from the northern army at Albany. Otherwise, though, the game was "pretty well up" in early December. Washington was back across the Delaware. Save for the absence of boats, which Washington had had the forethought to collect up and down the river, there was nothing to stop the British from marching in strength upon Philadelphia. Morale in the middle colonies was understandably low, and not improved when Congress – acting upon advice from Generals Israel Putnam and Thomas Mifflin – withdrew from Philadelphia to Baltimore. Charles Lee in a careless reconnaissance was taken prisoner by a British patrol. The militia were deserting in numbers, and the Continental enlistments were about to expire.

But somehow the crisis was averted. Howe called off large-scale operations for the winter and dispatched six thousand men under Clinton to occupy Newport, Rhode Island. By the offer of bounties some troops were persuaded to re-enlist. Two thousand militia were sent forward from Philadelphia.

Above all, Washington rose to the occasion with a brilliant coup at Trenton, during Christmas night. His plan was to take three parties across the half-frozen Delaware and surprise the British outposts on the far bank. In more ambitious form, it was reminiscent of his dawn assault of Jumonville's camp, back in 1754. The scheme was admirably conceived, and though two of the three columns were unable to negotiate the river, the principal one – led by Washington – succeeded. The garrison of fifteen hundred Hessians in Trenton was overwhelmed after a brief struggle, though five hundred managed to slip away. Their performance was abject, no doubt because some of them had drunk too much in celebration of Christmas. Still, that is not to gainsay the high daring of Washington's attack, or the boldness of his further stroke, a week later. Having again crossed the Delaware, he was almost trapped by Cornwallis, but nimbly extricated himself, fighting a successful skirmish at Princeton on the way.

It would be hard to exaggerate the importance of these ventures in their effect upon patriotic morale or upon Washington's own reputation. On January 17, 1777, Nicholas Cresswell was at Leesburg, Virginia. After talking with an acquaintance there, Cresswell noted in his journal:

> Six weeks ago this gentleman was lamenting the unhappy situation of the Americans and pitying the wretched condition of their much-beloved General, supposing his want of skill and experience in military matters had brought them all to the brink of destruction. In short, all was gone, all was lost. But now the scale is turned and Washington's name is extolled to the clouds. . . . It is the Damd Hessians that has caused this, curse the scoundrel that first thought of sending them here.

After Princeton, Washington remained quiet for the winter at his Morristown headquarters. Howe withdrew the Delaware outposts, concentrating his garrisons around New Brunswick. For both sides it was a period in which to take stock. We may do the same, first with references to the American position.

PROBLEMS AND POSSIBILITIES

Most of his early biographers have praised Washington's generalship, with little or no qualification. In fact, he made serious errors of judgment in the campaigns around New York. A British comment, at a later stage in the war, was that "any other General in the world other than General Howe would have beaten General Washington; and any other General in the world than General Washington would have beaten General Howe." It was a cheap jibe, and not a fair equation. Washington bore an appalling burden of responsibility. The inexperience of subordinate commanders magnified every minor mistake or hesitation on his part. Where Howe's professionals could interpret unclear orders, or themselves take the initiative at doubtful moments, Washington's amateur officers were apt to fail to read between the lines. With the forces at his disposal in 1776, Washington had practically no chance of defeating the British, but he did blunder. At Brooklyn Heights he made the mistake of reinforcing failure; a sharper opponent would not have allowed him the luxury of second thoughts. His subsequent movements were, though not panicky, indecisive and clumsy. The loss of Fort Washington, or rather of its large garrison and its precious cannon and supplies, was in part at least his fault.

Moreover, he was reluctant to acknowledge his mistakes. The line between righteousness and self-righteousness is always a narrow one; and Washington, though he had matured impressively since his Virginia colonel days, still showed a tendency to confuse the two. He suffered acutely when he was under criticism, or felt he might be. Over and over, in the letters he wrote during 1776, and again in 1777, he insisted that he did not object to fair criticism; yet, since only he and his close associates were fully aware of his "choice of difficulties," how could any criticism be fair? Desperately concerned for his "honor," he was still a shade too ready to shift the onus onto others. Thus, he was not quite just to his faithful general, Nathanael Greene, in his account of the Fort Washington surrender, though on subsequent occasions his treatment of Greene, Knox and other trusted officers was generous and considerate; and he was inclined to overstress his vexations at the hands of Congress.

Militarily, Washington still had much to learn. Temperamentally, he was something less than perfect. But he was capable of learning; and, in balance, his temperament was extremely well adapted to the task before him. In his initial lapses we may discern the source of his ultimate victories. For he was a fighter; he erred not through timidity, which would have proved fatal in the long run, but through pugnacity. It was bitter for him to accept the tactical necessity that America's weakness laid upon him: the necessity of avoiding a major engagement. But by degrees he reconciled himself to the truth that (as he wrote to Congress in September 1776) "on our Side the War should be defensive." His task henceforward was uncomfortable, and even inglorious, but at any rate it was becoming clear that he must survive, and with him an army, until the enemy wearied of the struggle. Fortunately, he was tenacious as well as pugnacious. The man who had persisted in his Virginia land claims for fifteen years was not likely to give up when so much more was at stake. This was the meaning of his sudden defiance at Trenton. He yearned for a more ambitious stroke, and his truculence at Princeton almost brought disaster. But the device by which he escaped from Cornwallis's army at Princeton showed how Washington was beginning to grasp the role of guerrilla general: he lit camp fires – and then, leaving them burning, slipped away in the darkness, just when Cornwallis was announcing jubilantly that he had caught "the old fox" and would "bag him in the morning."

We have said that he sometimes complained at Congress. Not without cause; its procedures were often tardy, inadequate, and even stupid. Some of the delegates were mediocre; and the level of merit sank as the war dragged on. Congress could, and should, have done more to provide a proper standing army, instead of the miscellany of Continentals and militia that formed the patriot armies. But its own difficulties were more formidable than Washington realized. The war was costly; the Continental currency became so debased that a loyalist newspaper in New York facetiously advertised for some on behalf of an English gentleman who wished to use it for wallpaper. If Washington was new to his responsibilities, so was Congress; and it had preoccupations – its negotiations with foreign countries, for example – with which Washington did not have to concern himself.

The point is that Congress treated Washington far better than some of his biographers have cared to admit. Its official relations with him were honest and courteous, and most of its members were on good terms with him. There was bound to be some friction where his authority and that of Congress could not be firmly distinguished. If Washington had been a more imperious commander in chief, there might have been serious disagreement. But in general he trusted and deferred to Congress, and Congress – we must emphasize – reciprocated. How else, even allowing for the nervousness of the moment, are we to account for Congress's extraordinary gesture in December 1776? For a period then unspecified – which turned out to be six months – it conferred almost dictatorial powers upon George Washington, as far as the raising and maintenance of his army were concerned. Indeed, he was commonly mentioned at the time as the "Dictator" – not always in a hostile sense – and some people, with or without the precedent of Oliver Cromwell in mind, spoke of him as "Lord Protector."

Congress and Washington had their problems; so had the British. At home they were divided in their allegiances and hence in their policies. There was decided opposition, in Parliament and elsewhere, to George III and his Tory advisers. The King himself had no doubt that the colonies must be restored to his realm, by force if reason failed – the iron hand in the velvet glove. But as the war dragged on, it seemed that the figure should be changed; what the British proffered was a mailed fist with a flabby hand within it. They held military and naval supremacy, yet seemed unable or unwilling to sue it decisively. It would be inaccurate to portray General Gage and his successors as a group of tender-hearted well-wishers, though neither were they (nor poor melancholy, conscientious George III) the supercilious monsters depicted in patriot propaganda. Their original mistake lay rather in despising than in secretly admiring the American colonists. "They are raw, undisciplined, cowardly men," declared Lord Sandwich in a much-publicized taunt; and Gage's frontal assault at Bunker Hill showed that he shared Sandwich's opinion – though not when the battle was over. Sir William Howe (he was knighted for having won at Long Island) was less sanguine, but he also conducted operations in 1776 with a degree of disdain.

To some extent though, his hesitations are explicable in terms of scruple. We may perhaps discount the fact that Gage had an American wife, that Clinton's father had been colonial governor of New York, that Howe's elder brother (killed at Ticonderoga in 1758, fighting the French) had been a hero in the colonies.

But we cannot overlook the fatal ambiguity of their endeavors. It is well summarized in the situation of the Howe brothers, who, when they came to New York to wage war on the rebels, in all the panoply of destruction, came also as peace commissioners, officially empowered by George III to discuss an "accommodation." After General Howe's success on Long Island, he delayed further operations in order to hold a parley with the enemy. He and Admiral Howe were to be employed again as commissioners in 1778, while still responsible for the conduct of the war. But their victories were too mild, and their terms too harsh.

In part, of course, the trouble lay with their lack of military genius. Britain had had a Blake, and was to produce a Nelson; it had had a Marlborough, and was to produce a Wellington. But Lord Howe, Graves, even Rodney were not Nelsons. Neither Gage nor "Billy" Howe nor Clinton nor "Gentleman Johnny" Burgoyne was a Wellington. This is not to say that they were altogether incompetent; nor was Lord George Germain, who as secretary of state for the colonies directed the war from London, as viciously silly as some commentators have asserted. All the British commanders in the field were moderately good soldiers, courageous, methodical, and skilled in the art of European warfare. The best of them, Cornwallis, had a highly successful subsequent career in other parts of the world. Their misfortune was that they were not great soldiers. They were not unperceptive; indeed, they were all too clearly aware of their problems. As in some old fairy tale, they were to be vouchsafed three chances — the first golden, the others increasingly tarnished — to end the war at a stroke. This first chance was given to Gage on Charlestown peninsula in June 1775. If he had been prudent in attacking Breed's Hill, and then bold in following up his opportunity, instead of the other way around, he might have shattered Artemas Ward's inchoate army before Washington ever arrived on the scene. The second chance was given to Howe on Long Island and afterward. If he had burst through Washington's defenses at Brooklyn Heights, or advanced more briskly in the subsequent pursuits, he might have destroyed the Continental army beyond redemption. He was to be given another, final chance in 1777.

Each time the odds grew longer. On the face of it, the British had all the advantages. Viewed more closely, their advantages seemed to dwindle. The war was costly, and unpopular at home. The navy, undermanned, was allotted more tasks around the world than it could carry out. The army likewise was under strength, and scattered across the globe; hence the need to hire troops from European princelings. Operations had to be developed three thousand miles from home; communications were slow and erratic; soldiers and sailors had not been trained to cooperate with one another. What confronted Howe and his associates was a kind of guerrilla war in an enormous land whose climate — sweltering to stark — taxed even the native Americans. It was a land of few roads, densely wooded outside the settlements; Washington, we may recall, had in 1754 taken fifteen days to cut his way twenty miles through the Allegheny forest. An implacable country — as it still strikes European travelers today.

Washington had his "choice of difficulties." Yet by the autumn of 1776 his duty, though desperately demanding, reduced itself to simple essentials. He must endure, evade, exhort. Howe in comparison had almost an excess of alternatives. With the aid of the navy he could descend on any part of the American seaboard; and though secrecy hardly appears to have been aimed at in the strategic planning of the period, it was not a vital factor. All the chief American cities lay at his mercy. Howe held Newport, from which he could threaten New England. Possession of New York, apart from protecting the considerable loyalist element in its population, enabled him to control access to Canada and the Great Lakes. If he could seize Philadelphia, the largest city in America and the seat of Congress, he might dominate the middle colonies; and the capture of Charleston might open the door to the South.

But what then? He could not occupy every American seaport simultaneously; and even if that were possible, it would not quell the rebellion. There would remain the intolerable expanse of wilderness, the long marches, the thankless chase, the risk of ambush by an enemy that did not abide by the orthodox rules of war – did not know that there *were* rules. There would remain the unnumerable settlements, most of them yet unrecorded by the mapmaker. Washington himself was a countryman, the product of a large state without a single city in it. Perhaps it was thereby easier for him to envisage his true role. Howe preferred to traverse ground and garrison cities rather than harry the Continental troops. He had his reasons, of which a taste for comfort – snug quarters and a charming mistress – was only one and not the most important one. He could not afford heavy losses, or to lose his army in driblets. American forces might be scattered, but they could reunite; more men would be forthcoming. Howe's troops were expensive commodities, to be husbanded. So he argued – wrongly. His subordinate, Sir Henry Clinton (who also collected a knighthood), was wiser, at any rate in theory, in urging Howe to strike at Washington. But Clinton in practice was not an aggressive warrior. Moreover, he and Howe were congenitally opposed, so that each tended to frustrate the other's schemes. "By some cursed fatality," Clinton was to confess in July 1777, "we could never draw together."

Behind their mutual irritation lay the reflection that they were waging a civil war, with all the tragic, queasy discord that such strife entails. Should they be ruthless, and make themselves, the more hated? Should they be magnanimous, and be ridiculed for their pains? In this particular sense, they came by stages to realize, they could never entirely win. Perhaps there *was* no definable objective, except to dispose of Washington himself. No wonder the rumor was so often spread that Washington had been taken prisoner – pure wish fulfillment. There was a plot to kill Washington in 1776; from the British point of view it was an excellent idea. (Charles Lee, the other highly esteemed American commander in 1776, actually was made prisoner in December of that year, but with no very evident results. No general on either side, except Washington, was regarded by many people as indispensable. When later a raid was proposed, to kidnap Clinton, the project was criticized on the score that a better general might be sent out from England to replace him.)

If Washington ever had a bad dream – he left no record of one – it might well have been that he was at sea in a small vessel whose sail was made of paper (his army; the precarious union of colonies, not even enrolled under a system of government until the Articles of Confederation were finally ratified in 1781); the rain came – and the sail dissolved. If ever Howe had a bad dream – which is quite conceivable – it might have been similar, except that the ship was large, and the sail made of stout canvas; there came a storm; the sail blew loose – and Howe had not enough hands to fasten it down again. In short, Washington's plight was to defend a continent without substantial enough means; Howe's fate was to attack it when – once the rebellion gathered momentum – no means could be quite sufficient. The British were to demonstrate, as others have done since, how hard it is to suppress a popular rising in a big country if the inhabitants have any pride of spirit. Napoleon in turn was to make the discovery in the Spanish peninsula and again, more disastrously, in Russia; the Boer republics were to hold out for three years against Britain; the Germans were to learn the lesson in occupied Europe.

CRISIS AND CABAL: 1777-1778

For the meantime, though, Howe's prospects for 1777 were fairly rosy. In the early spring, while Washington was moving forward his army out of winter quarters, Howe was considering various schemes. His first impulse was, not to meet Washington's modest challenge, but to join forces at Albany with an expedition to be sent south from Canada. This scheme, which also involved an attack on Boston from Rhode Island, he submitted to the colonial secretary, Germain. Then Howe changed his mind and advocated an advance on Philadelphia, together with a limited offensive northward from New York City by a smaller army. Germain preferred the second plan on the grounds of economy; hardly any reinforcements were available and Howe said he would need an additional fifteen thousand men to implement the previous plan. Germain was also influenced by Burgoyne, who had returned to England on leave for the winter. Angling for an independent command, Burgoyne convinced Germain that he had a master stroke to propose: a converging advance upon the focal point of Albany by two forces – with Burgoyne himself at the head – from the north, out of Montreal. Germain also sanctioned this scheme.

Here the inadequacies in the British system of command became crucial. As befitted one who was an amateur playwright, Burgoyne's plan had a certain dramatic symmetry. But like its author's literary productions it was, while imposing in conception, weak in detail. It paid little heed to the problems of co-ordinating two separate attacks, or of movement and supply in the rough terrain between Montreal and Albany. It assumed that merely to arrive in Albany was to have won a major victory: New England would be isolated; the colonies would be carved into segments like some succulent turkey. But would they? Could the British keep their communications open; could they possibly hope to prevent American parties from moving across the extended line?

Howe's amended plan was superior, if it meant dealing with Washington's army. There, if anywhere, lay the heart of the rebellion. During the spring and early summer Cornwallis attempted rather perfunctorily to get to grips with Washington. But the latter was by now too skilled in adversity to accept the challenge, and dodged away.

Howe in the interim changed his mind again. His new idea was to capture Philadelphia by sea, in a great naval operation for which he set aside fifteen thousand of his best troops. This meant that no regulars could be spared for a push north from New York City, only some loyalist bands with vague injunctions to be active. The aim of the convergence on Albany remained unclear; and instead of pinning the northern American army, Burgoyne ran the risk of being trapped himself. But Howe was set on Philadelphia, and too engrossed in the complex logistics of that enterprise to listen to the protests of Clinton, who was to be left in New York. Neither Burgoyne nor Germain learned of the altered emphasis of Howe's intentions until it was too late. Even then Germain did not worry unduly; he was content to order Howe to support Burgoyne as soon as Philadelphia was taken.

It is not surprising that these British contrivances mystified Washington; their logic was hard to follow. But it gradually became clear to him that the enemy had two main ends in view: to invade from Canada, and to invade the middle or southern colonies by sea. Washington was able to guess fairly accurately at the numbers involved. Burgoyne, with eight thousand men, could be dealt with by the northern army. Clinton, with seven thousand (only half of them regulars), could do no more than skirmish from his New York base, unless he showed unwonted energy. Washington was therefore free to parry Howe. He would be outnumbered, but not hopelessly so, for by midsummer he had some nine thousand Continentals, plus an indefinite quantity of local militia. "If the Enemy will give us time to collect an Army levied for the War," Washington wrote to Benedict Arnold in February 1777, "I hope we shall set all our former Errors to rights." He did not get more than a fraction of what he wanted; although Congress offered bounties of money and land to men who would enlist in the

Continental service for three years or the duration of the war, these terms were less attractive than the bounties offered by individual states to their own militia for shorter service within their own boundaries. The Continental army was to remain dismayingly small. Yet it did provide Washington with a solid nucleus of seasoned soldiers. And while they and the militia looked unkempt, appearances were deceptive. Thanks to surreptitious aid from France and Spain, captured British supplies and their own improvised manufactures, the American troops were moderately well armed and clothed.

The enemy also gave Washington ample time. Howe's armada did not sail out of New York Harbor until late July, and did not disembark for a whole month after that. Howe came ashore at Head of Elk, in Chesapeake Bay, farther than he need have been from Philadelphia. Still, once he was on the move, he acted confidently, skirmishing toward the city by steady stages. Washington had been baffled by Howe's preliminary motions, not understanding why a general who was only sixty miles away from Philadelphia at New Brunswick should make a four-hundred-mile sea voyage in order to be seventy miles away at the end of it. He believed that Howe's objective must be Charleston. But it was, he discovered, Philadelphia after all; and Howe's journey took so long that Washington was able to forestall him and to interpose the American army between Howe and his goal.

So far, fortune smiled on Washington. In the next few weeks, the dice rolled against him – and, as in previous campaigns, he had himself to blame somewhat. Unless he stood fast and fought, he was certain to lose Philadelphia. Though that would not spell utter defeat, it would, he wrote, "strike . . . a damp" to the American cause. It was his duty, therefore, to face Howe; and in this sense Howe's scheme was not altogether futile. Washington was outnumbered – eleven thousand to fifteen thousand – but he could choose the ground for an encounter. The place he selected was a few miles from Wilmington, where the Brandywine Creek crossed his front. This was on September 10. Washington entrusted his right wing to Sullivan (who had been exchanged after capture on Long Island), the center to Nathanael Green, and the left flank to the Pennsylvania militia. The Brandywine could be forded at several points, but otherwise formed a useful natural obstacle, especially on the American left.

Howe's plan of attack was similar to that at Brooklyn: a feint against the American center while the main thrust was delivered on the flank – the right flank on this occasion. It was his standard procedure, and Washington was slow in not anticipating it, or even arranging a screen of scouts. The result was that the battle opened on September 11 with inconclusive clashes in the center, to cover a long sweep round the flank by Cornwallis. His ten thousand men caught Sullivan unprepared and dislodged the American right wing. Washington made the best of the situation by sending most of his remaining troops, under Greene, to establish a second line behind Sullivan's retreating divisions. Greene's troops, fighting stubbornly, held on till dark. Meanwhile, the center, denuded to support the flank, collapsed under Howe's pressure. The battle lost its shape; at dusk, as the firing died down, weary men straggled back in disarray, leaving about a thousand of their comrades dead and wounded on the field.

It was a defeat and a more costly one than need have been incurred. But it was by no means a decisive defeat. A cynical observer might note that few American prisoners were taken; they ran away too fast. It could be said, in reply, that they ran just far enough; by the next morning they were regrouping in their old units. And those who held firm with Greene gave an excellent account of themselves, since the British suffered over five hundred casualties. In other words, if the Americans were still not able to worst a British army in a formal battle, they showed that they could combine the agility of guerrillas (in retreat, it is true) with the steadiness of regulars – not in an ideal combination, yet with sufficient resourcefulness to avert disaster.

What followed repeated the pattern, with the addition of the special quality of belligerence that Washington always revealed at critical moments when he felt America's future – and his own reputation – was at stake. Howe plodded toward Philadelphia; Congress hastily departed to Lancaster and then to York, Pennsylvania; Washington essayed another battle, which was canceled by heavy rain; Howe entered the city; Washington challenged him at Germantown, ten miles outside Philadelphia. This time there was a battle, a confused one in which Washington's audacity was ill rewarded by the loss again of a thousand men at half that cost to his adversary, Washington's reaction was to risk another battle, but Howe would not again oblige him. With December came the winter – another winter of mild uneasiness for the British and of active discontent among the patriots. While Howe was warm in Philadelphia, Washington's men had to keep watch outside, twenty miles away along the Schuylkill on a bleak plateau at Valley Forge. The settlements around Philadelphia were already so crowded with refugees that Washington felt he could not find ready-made accommodation for his soldiers. The army had therefore to survive under canvas until it could construct its own wooden encampment. Several cold, starved weeks elapsed, thanks in large part to the incompetence of Thomas Mifflin's commissariat, before Washington and his men were housed. Even then, there was still for some while an acute lack of food and clothing. The suffering at Valley Forge has for good reason entered into the lore of American national sentiment. Not all those who evoke its somber name stress the accompanying element of irony. The suffering, that is, could to a considerable extent have been avoided. As Washington well knew, and as he bitterly observed in his correspondence, the shivering ill-fed troops in the cabins at Valley Forge had more to endure from the neglect of their fellow Americans than from the attentions of their British enemies.

Nevertheless, the patriot balance sheet, during the winter of 1777-1778, did not look bad. On the debit side was the broad factor of Howe's seizure of Philadelphia, with the parenthetical setbacks of Brandywine and Germantown. On the credit side Washington's army was still in being, though weakened and disgruntled by cold weather, niggardly supplies and arrears in pay. While his army dwindled almost to nothing each winter, that was offset by the British habit of hibernating. Congress likewise dwindled amid the discomforts of York, until its sessions were sometimes attended by fewer than twenty members; yet it too was still in existence. The sap ran back into the tree; the tree did not die. As for Howe, his expedition was a failure, because it was not a triumph. He had expected that the loyalists would rally to his banner; but while the Pennsylvanians were ready to sell him provisions – taking his gold where they refused the Continental currency – only a handful actually joined him. Despondent, Howe sent in his resignation.

More positively, the "Northern Department" had won a resounding victory over Burgoyne. Burgoyne's invasion started ominously for the Americans with the capture of Fort Ticonderoga in early July. But thereafter his advance was slow and painful; and the secondary invasion along the Mohawk, despite initial success, fizzled out. In mid-August a portion of Burgoyne's force, in search of sorely needed supplies, was annihilated by patriot militia at Bennington in southern Vermont. He had no alternative but to press south to Albany, even though he learned that there would be no army from New York City to meet him. He was brought to a halt a few miles south of Saratoga by the northern army (formerly commanded by Schuyler and now under Horatio Gates). In September and again in early October he tried in vain to break out. Worried by the imminent catastrophe, Clinton at last responded by sailing up the Hudson with as many men as he could spare. By the middle of October, pushing aside resistance, he was at Esopus

(Kingston), only eighty miles from Burgoyne. But Clinton was as cautious as Burgoyne had been rash; he came too late and – thanks to Howe's obsession with Philadelphia – brought too few with him. The day after Clinton's vanguard reached Esopus, Burgoyne at Saratoga surrendered what was left of his army: fifty-seven hundred men. It was a sensational reverse for British arms. Clinton retired to New York, to remain there quietly through the winter. Howe, also inert, waited in Philadelphia until his resignation was accepted; then, in May 1778, he handed over his command in America to Clinton and went home. Gage had gone, Burgoyne, Howe. Washington was outlasting them all.

The moral was not lost on Europe. In London, Lord North began to arrange another peace commission, though Britain was not yet prepared to recognize the independence of the colonies. In Paris there was intense activity. In conjunction with Silas Deane and Benjamin Franklin – the American agents in Paris – the French government had for some time been aiding the colonies. Part of their aid consisted in sending over foreign officers to serve with Washington, and some came on their own initiative. The majority were a doubtful asset and added to Washington's troubles, since they expected high rank. But some – notably Thaddeus Kosciuszko, the eager young Marquis de Lafayette, baron de Kalb and "Baron" von Steuben (of spurious nobility but a genuine solider) – were of great value to the American cause. On the news of Saratoga, the French decided to do much more. Their decision was not based on sentiment, though they admired the courage of the colonies and the firmness of Washington, the commander in chief. It rested on a hardheaded estimate of America's chances and – above all – on the prospect of weakening Britain. Hence the readiness, which France's ally Spain deplored, of a despotic monarchy to come to the aid of a struggling republic. In a letter sent at the end of February 1778, Franklin was able to announce that "the most Christian king agrees to make a common cause with the United States . . . [and] guarantees their liberty, sovereignty, and independence, absolute and unlimited." By mid-summer France was officially at war with England. Spain followed suit a year later, though she would not go as far as the French in recognizing the United States as a separate nation.

Washington heard of the treaty in April. "I believe no event," he wrote to Congress, "was ever received with more heartfelt joy," and no one was more relieved himself. Oddly enough, the weeks during which the alliance was being formulated were among the worst in Washington's whole life. To the physical misery of the log huts at Valley Forge was added a good deal of mental anguish, for this was the period of the so-called Conway Cabal – a plot to oust Washington from the supreme command in favor of Horatio Gates.

We shall probably never know the exact truth of the affair. As Washington saw it, a number of malcontents in the army combined with others in Congress in a secret program to discredit him. The military ringleaders appeared to be Gates, Mifflin and Thomas Conway (an Irish volunteer, formerly a colonel in the French service). According to the familiar story, their machinations were exposed by faithful supporters of Washington (including Lafayette, who had become his ardent admirer and friend); Washington then confronted Gates with evidence of the plot, and thereby so abashed the conspirators that they abandoned their dark projects. However, Bernhard Knollenberg and other recent scholars have questioned the orthodox version. They point out that it was natural enough at the time to praise Gates, who had vanquished Burgoyne and to be correspondingly less enthusiastic – for the moment – over Washington, who had been worsted by Howe. Perhaps Gates did not deserve so much acclaim, nor Washington so much blame. But that is the way with popular esteem, especially in war; the lucky generals are usually promoted, the unlucky ones shelved. It may have been ungrateful to grumble at Washington; was it, though, less majesty for a few of his associates to discuss his shortcomings in private letters to one another? Conway was self-seeking, and perhaps not even sincere at that, when he wrote to Gates that he preferred him to Washington; was he a monster? Washington apparently thought so, and most of his biographers have agreed, putting themselves not only in his shoes (as a biographer should) but also in his pocket (which is a blind devotion). In consequence they have tended to accept as given data the notion that Gates and the rest behaved treasonably, that Gates was incompetent as well as disloyal, and that Congress was composed almost entirely of knaves and fools.

In fairness to Washington we must admit that his friends spoke as though there *were* an actual conspiracy. "I cannot doubt its reality in the most extensive sense," wrote Colonel Alexander Hamilton. True, some members of Congress *were* malicious and irresponsible. "There is as much intrigue in this State-House as in the Vatican," John Jay complained. And there *was* a great deal of back-biting among Washington's senior officers. But that is always found where men compete for honor and advancement – witness the ill feeling between Clinton, Howe and Burgoyne. If Washington had been one of several major generals, instead of in the lofty office of commander in chief, would even he have been immune to the pangs of jealousy? As it was, though his conduct in relation to the cabal was dignified, and certainly effective, he was almost excessively angered by it. For months he was still furious with Gates – and Congress was wise in making sure that the two men were kept widely apart.

MONMOUTH TO YORKTOWN: 1778-1781

Plot or no, the trouble was soon overlaid by more urgent considerations. In June 1778, to Washington's amazement, Clinton marched his redcoats out of Philadelphia, not to fight but head northeast across New Jersey. He was not insane – he had never liked Howe's plan; few reinforcements were promised from England; there was a report that a French fleet was on the way; hence he preferred to concentrate his forces in New York City. So, like Boston two years before, Philadelphia was relinquished to the Americans. The mere evacuation was a moral victory for the United States. Washington, breaking camp at Valley Forge, followed in Clinton's wake, determined to drive home the lesson.

His opportunity came on the morning of June 28, as Clinton's rearguard was moving off from Monmouth Court House. It was Sunday, a day of ovenlike heat. Washington's orders to the vanguard of the American army were to accost the British and bring on a battle. This task he entrusted to Charles Lee, who had been taken prisoner in December 1776 and only just released, on exchange. The two armies were fairly equal in strength, and Washington held the tactical advantage of having the enemy drawn out on the move. But the eccentric Lee seemingly disapproved of the scheme. He advanced without much conviction and retreated without much skill when Clinton swiftly brought up reinforcements. Washington, alarmed and then annoyed, halted Lee's withdrawal and patched up his front. No full-scale battle developed, however, and that night, when each side had suffered about three hundred fifty casualties, Clinton's redcoats continued their methodical progress to New York. Embarking at Sandy Hook, they completed the journey by sea. Washington's chance was gone, and the subsequent court-martial of Lee (who was deemed guilty of serious insubordination and suspended from active command for the rest of the war) did nothing to sweeten the fact. But, apart from all else that might be said about the encounter at Monmouth, it offered one more proof of Washington's aggressive spirit. It was not simply that he revealed again, as conspicuously as at Trenton or Germantown, his personal courage under fire. It was that – against the advice of his council of war – he tried to bring on a major battle. His motive may have been quite practical, since he suspected that the New Jersey militia would desert him (which they did immediately afterward) to go and gather in their crops. Or he may have felt that the American morale "stood in need of something to keep us afloat" (a phrase he used some time later). Whatever his reasons, the interesting feature is his eagerness to commit his army in a formal engagement.

In retrospect we can see that the French alliance was the turning point of the war. Once the British were at grips with their old enemy, and with Spain, their naval supremacy was challenged; thus, they could not prevent a French fleet under the Comte d'Estaing from sailing for America in 1778. Elsewhere they were hard pressed – in the Mediterranean, where Gibraltar was besieged, in the West Indies, and as far away as the Indian Ocean. They had to face the possibility (though it never matured) of a Franco-Spanish invasion of Britain. In December 1780 Holland joined Britain's enemies; and in the same year, led by Russia, a number of European countries demonstrated their hostility by banding together in a League of Armed Neutrality.

In retrospect again, we can see Valley Forge as the nadir of the American effort. Henceforward, Washington's primacy as military leader was unquestioned. The third and final hope of routing him lay with Howe at Germantown and Brandywine – or perhaps in a sudden midwinter assault upon Valley Forge. When Howe settled for minor successes, there was never to be another time at which Washington, or the cause he stood for, could be smashed at a blow. Now, if the French were as good as their word, the prospect of victory and independence for the United States was not far over the horizon.

It would make a neater story if all had gone well for Washington after Valley Forge. But it is only hindsight that permits us to speak so optimistically. When Washington continued his march from Monmouth, circling New York City to take up position at White Plains, his army, geographically, stood where it had two whole years before. Weeks, months, years were dragging by. To talk of horizons did not bring much consolation when the way ahead seemed so interminable. Martha had been able to spend part of each winter with him, in company with a few other senior officers' wives at headquarters. For instance, she joined him at Valley Forge in early February. But Mount Vernon, where his cousin Lund Washington was in charge, must have appeared infinitely remote. It was often in his thoughts; even at unlikely moments we find him dropping his official concerns for a while to send instructions on experiments in agriculture, or additions to be made to the house ("How many Lambs have you had this Spring? . . . Have you any prospect of getting paint and Oyl? Are you going to repair the Pavement of the Piazza? . . . Have you made any attempts to reclaim more Land for meadow?"). Over and over in his letters he recurs wistfully to the dream of reposing under his "own vine and fig tree," as though that particular Biblical phrase summed up for him everything that life held of contentment.

There was, by contrast, little tranquility in the immediate scene. The French alliance made heartening news, but its first effect in America was disappointing. D'Estaing's fleet duly arrived, in July 1778. Since New York City was too tough a nut to crack, Washington arranged for the French to combine with an American force led by Sullivan in an attack on the British garrison at Rhode Island. D'Estaing, however, was tackled by a British fleet and eventually retired to the West Indies, while, deprived of naval support, Sullivan failed to overcome the garrison. It was not an auspicious start to the alliance. Clearly, coalition warfare posed a whole set of fresh problems which would require all Washington's ingenuity and tact to solve. A French fleet would be merely on loan; it would be extremely difficult to concert plans far in advance; strategic decisions would now have to take into account not only Congress but also the views of the French court and the French commanders in America.

Indeed, Washington feared that the intervention of France might lead to a fatal relaxation of effort on the part of his countrymen. As enemies, the Americans' own apathy and inefficiency were almost as dangerous as all of Clinton's redcoats. Or so it seemed to Washington, who – it must be remembered – spent most of his time not in fighting but in dealing with an endless series of administrative crises. His correspondence was so enormous that, at times he employed several secretaries; and the greater part of what he wrote had to do with food, weapons, ammunition, clothing, blankets, horses, pay (invariably in arrears), requisitioning, recruiting, promotions (and refusals to promote), punishments, bounties, militia quotas and the like. He felt that such labors could be much reduced if Congress, the states and individual Americans would only pull their weight. It is possible that he complained too much and that he exaggerated a little the extent of the army's various shortages – like any shrewd claimant who does not expect to get all that he asks for and therefore asks for more than he can actually make do with. Even so, he was not exaggerating much when – as late as April 1781 – he could declare that "we are at the end of our tether." From his standpoint the winter at Valley Forge was in some respects less critical than those of 1778-1779 and 1779-1780, each of which had led to small mutinies by a portion of the Continental line. Nathanael Greene bore the same ominous testimony from the South, in January 1781: "Unless this army is better supported than I see any prospect of, the Country [i.e., the South?] is lost beyond redemption."

"There was not much pleasure thar," Martha confessed to her brother-in-law in her ingenuous prose, shortly after returning home from "the Camp" at Morristown in July 1780 – "the distress of the army and other difficulty tho' I did not know the cause" made her husband, "the pore General . . . so unhappy that it distressed me exceedingly."

It is understandable that Washington became increasingly bitter against both the British and their Tory supporters in America. Who was loyal? Clinton and Washington, each with equal justification in his own eyes, gave opposite answers. To one a Tory was a patriot, potentially; to the other, a traitor. Washington thought of his own well-developed intelligence service as a legitimate auxiliary arm, but viewed Clinton's similar activities as sinister and underhand; and vice versa. Clinton was disappointed by the weakness of the Tory response, though Simcoe's Rangers and other loyalist bodies rendered him valuable service; Washington was disgusted by the extent of hidden Tory sympathy. Treason lurked everywhere. No one knew for certain whether Charles Lee had been "corrupted" while he was a prisoner; had he not been borne off by a patrol from the 16th Light Dragoons – his old regiment as a British officer, and Howe's? Patrick Henry was so disturbed by the mood of Virginia in June 1778 that he wrote to one of the state's delegates in Congress, "For God's sake, my dear sir, quit not the councils of your country, until you see us forever disjoined from Great Britain. *The old leaven still works. The flesh pots of Egypt are still savoury to degenerate palates.*" His words took on a prophetic ring two years later when Benedict Arnold – the most dashing officer in the American army, the hero of Quebec and Saratoga – was detected while preparing to betray the Hudson defenses at West Point to Clinton. Arnold escaped; even worse, lavishly rewarded, he became a British brigadier general and carried out destructive raids in Connecticut and Virginia. With an asperity rare in him, Washington hanged Major André, the attractive young British officer who – acting under Clinton's orders – was Arnold's go-between, and whose capture revealed the plot.

Hard times: words like "mortification," "embarrassment" and "misfortune" come readily to Washington's pen in the long interlude after the midsummer day at Monmouth. This was true of campaigns as well as of life in camp. The Americans did score some minor successes on land, while John Paul Jones and other captains in their infant navy came off best in several small engagements. None of these, however, made much difference to the general tenor of the war. The British concentrated their effort in the South, evacuating Newport at the end of 1780 to employ its garrison more profitably elsewhere. They had seized Savannah, in Georgia, a year earlier; and in the autumn of 1780 Clinton brought an army by sea to Charleston and laid siege to it. His operations were cumbersome, but they achieved the desired result. Charleston fell, and with it, in the most costly setback of the war, a force of over five thousand American defenders. Clinton returned to New York, leaving Cornwallis with eight thousand men to hold Georgia and South Carolina as a loyalist bastion. Washington, compelled to remain on the Hudson and watch Clinton, did what he could by dispatching all the troops he could spare to the South; and Congress sent Horatio Gates to take command there.

Now at last the struggle quickened dramatically in tempo. Over thousands of miles the main actors, unwitting, began to make the moves that would draw them all together for the final act. The lesser protagonists, deservedly or not, were shouldered aside as irrelevant. Some had been prominent hitherto – Gates, for example. But he was heavily defeated by Cornwallis at Camden, South Carolina, in August 1780, and was superseded within three months. Out, too, goes the worthy Baron de Kalb, mortally wounded at Camden. Charles Lee is already relegated to the wings. Clinton, fretting but immobile in New York has few more lines to say – a "shy bitch" as he diagnosed himself, he is not one of history's lucky generals.

The remaining cast is headed by five figures, with others (Greene, Steuben and so on) in subsidiary roles. The five are Cornwallis, Lafayette, Washington and two late-comers – the Comte de Rochambeau and Admiral de Grasse.

Cornwallis brought on the dénouement through his winter campaign of 1780-1781. Ironically, it was a very able campaign. He was swift, he was resourceful, and he adapted his tactics to American conditions. He and his associate, the cavalry leader Banister Tarleton, humbled Gates at Camden and struck hard at Greene (in March 1781, at Guilford Court House). Yet Cornwallis writ in water. Behind him, as he hastened north, south again, and north once more, resistance rose afresh. By May he was in Virginia, where Tarleton almost captured Governor Thomas Jefferson and the startled state legislature. Cornwallis was bold, even brilliant. But he was doomed when, having failed to dispose of agile American forces led by Lafayette and Steuben, he decided to make for the coast and put himself in touch with Clinton. He chose Yorktown. Cornwallis had overreached himself. In previous campaigns Howe had failed through excess of prudence and Burgoyne through lack of it. If Clinton resembled Howe in this respect, Cornwallis ran the risk of being (as a contemporary remarked) "completely Burgoyned." Yorktown was not an easy place to defend and Cornwallis had fewer than eight thousand men.

Washington had endured three years of the times that try men's souls, then three more of the kind that tried men's patience and their pocketbooks. Now came the test of his capacity to seize a heaven-sent opportunity, to accomplish what, with too little strength, he had half essayed on other fields – a concerted maneuver by "the allied arms on this Continent . . . to effectuate once for all the great objects of the alliance." The opportunity arose through Rochambeau and De Grasse. The former, a good-natured, capable soldier, was at Newport with five thousand French troops. The latter, in command of the French West Indies fleet, announced that his ships, plus three thousand more French soldiers, would be available for a limited period, and that he was sailing for Chesapeake Bay.

Washington had been meditating an attack on New York with Rochambeau. He changed his mind on hearing from De Grasse and marched off toward Virginia. For the first time since Dorchester Heights, everything went smoothly for him, as though all the participants had rehearsed beforehand. De Grasse reached the jaws of Chesapeake Bay just ahead of a British squadron, sealing off Cornwallis's seaward exit. Within a few days Washington, Rochambeau, Lafayette and De Grasse converged and met. Seventeen thousand allied troops (eight thousand of them French) surrounded Yorktown and for the moment the French held naval supremacy. It was a miracle made actual. It was even being enacted in Washington's own setting; only a few miles away was Williamsburg, where half a lifetime ago he had ridden back from the Ohio country to warn Dinwiddie of the encroachments of the *fleur-de-lis*. In September and October 1781 he was well content to have the *fleur-de-lis* ranged alongside the "thirteen stripes alternate red and white," the "thirteen stars white in a blue field."

His Continentals strove to emulate the professionalism of the French: days of punctilio to round off the tatterdemalion years. Allied guns and mortars hammered the town. Outnumbered by two to one, and thwarted by a storm in an attempt to escape across the York River to Gloucester Point, Cornwallis lost heart. With an anguish that may be imagined, he sent a brief note to Washington on October 17 – the third anniversary of Saratoga:

SIR,

I propose a cessation of hostilities for twenty-four hours, and that two officers may be appointed by each side . . . to settle terms for the surrender of the posts at York and Gloucester.

I have the honor to be, &c

CORNWALLIS

Instead of "honour" he might more descriptively have substituted one of the words of Washington's lean years – "mortification," "embarrassment," "misfortune." For General Washington the drama was at the moment of splendid climax, as the British and the Hessians filed out, battalion after battalion, their standards furled, to lay down their arms. At this moment we should be able to terminate the tale, while the whole world (including even the British) applauded him.

But – never was a narrative so full of buts – it was not yet the end. As anticlimax, there were to be two more years of tedious epilogue, while the war slowly expired in an atmosphere of mingled exuberance, doubt and recrimination. The pleasure of Yorktown was overshadowed by the death of Washington's stepson, Jackie Custis, who had caught "camp-fever" there while serving as an aide-de-camp. The satisfaction Washington derived from the sterling performance of his Continentals in that last siege was marred in the next months as his army began to grumble and accuse. Others, the Continentals argued, had profiteered while they starved. Having won liberty for the United States, why must they have to plead with Congress for back pay? Responsible both to Congress and to his soldiers, with whom he had every sympathy, Washington had to summon all his tact to soothe his angry officers. Had they beaten the British only to come to blows with one another?

However, the war *was* won. There was no more serious fighting after Yorktown. Clinton, whose fleet had arrived too late with reinforcements for Cornwallis, went back uselessly to New York as he had done after Saratoga. Before long, treading the same path as Howe, he resigned and sailed for England. The remainder of the tale, for the British forces, was drab; little by little they packed their bags, evacuated their ports and fortresses and sailed away. The center of interest had shifted to Paris, where the American commissioners – John Adams, Franklin, Jay and Laurens – were getting an even better bargain than they had hoped. The independence of the United States was recognized, and her territories were defined as stretching from the seaboard to the Mississippi, from the Great Lakes to Spanish Florida. This handsome treaty was formally ratified by Congress in September 1783.

The war was won, the peace was won. When Washington accepted command in June 1775, he had written consolingly to Martha that he expected to "return safe to you in the fall." Privately he may have suspected that the call to duty would last much longer. He can hardly have supposed that it would last for eight and a half years. He was heartily glad to be homeward bound. But he could not make the transition and take "my leave of all the employments of public life" without deep emotion; too much had happened in the interim. Saying good-by to his officers at Fraunces' Tavern in New York, in December 1783, he and they were in tears; and when Washington handed back his commander in chief's commission to Congress at Annapolis a few days later, the significance, the weight of the occasion overwhelmed the spectators. There was too much to be said — an almost unbearable sense of history made and in the making. It lingered over Washington, in American minds, as he rode away, hurrying to be at Mount Vernon by Christmas Eve.

THE COMMANDER IN CHIEF'S ACHIEVEMENT

Where does he stand as a military leader? How, discounting malice and adulation alike, can we form a fair estimate of his accomplishments? The kind of war he was engaged in does not permit useful comparisons to be drawn with the renowned campaigns of history. It was one in which the Americans lost most of the battles, except the last, and in which none of the battles was on a giant scale. In the field, so far as we can judge, Washington did not show genius though his opportunities were limited.

Perhaps he may more justly be compared, not with Alexander, Frederick or Napoleon, but with fellow countrymen in another, subsequent American civil war. His military talent would not seem as fanatical as that of Stonewall Jackson, or as complete as that of Robert E. Lee. Unlike Lee, or McClellan, he did not inspire enthusiastic affection among the rank and file. Stirred by the writings of Tom Paine, who hated aristocracy, he could nevertheless insist that only "gentlemen" were fit to be officers; and it was the officers who admired him most. He lacked the common touch; it is significant that no one, not even on the British side, contrived a nickname for him. In the company of his equals, after dinner, he could thaw out most agreeably, as he sat sipping wine and eating nuts, which were his favorite dessert. But he cracked nuts, not jokes; and to the ordinary soldiers he was a stern, awe-inspiring figure. He attended to their wants, he shared their dangers and discomforts, but he was not one of them. He kept a distance, and emphasized it in a host of orders of the day that have a rigid, monitory sound; they are full of rebuke and prohibition, and where they are appreciative they are still a little glacial. They do not *give* praise; they *bestow* it.

It would be silly to stretch this point, and expect an eighteenth-century Virginia planter to behave like a twentieth-century expert in public relations. Yet he did strike even his contemporary associates as a reserved person. The war meant everything to him, but he did not – verbally speaking – rise to its major occasions. When the news of Saratoga reached him, he was having his portrait painted by Charles Willson Peale. "Ah," said Washington, reading the dispatch, "Burgoyne is defeated" – and continued to sit. Nothing more. And when Cornwallis surrendered, Washington detailed one of his aides to notify Congress, instead of composing the message himself. This goes beyond the laconic to a disappointing flatness.

However, these are hardly serious shortcomings, as we may see by looking again at that other American general named George: George B. McClellan, who for a while during the Civil War was also credited with having saved the Union. Both men were curiously compounded of humility and confidence. McClellan's, however, were misplaced. He was a notable trainer of armies – better than Washington (although the latter did not lean as heavily on Steuben as legend would have it). But McClellan was not a notable fighter. He displayed humility in face of the enemy and confidence to the point of arrogance where his chiefs or colleagues were concerned. A gifted man, he was nevertheless nervous and messianic, by turns. Washington, on the other hand, was a fighter who, with rare exceptions, kept the issue clear in his own mind. When he erred as a soldier, it was on the side or rashness; knowing this, with the deep self-knowledge that he somehow expected others to share, he was incensed by the imputation of timidity. Others might talk of Fabian tactics, even approvingly; he himself seems never to have invoked the name Fabius Cunctator, the Delayer.

He was not a perfect soldier, then; yet in Washington was discovered someone who came near to meeting an impossible list of requirements. Congress wanted first a commander in chief who would confer luster upon their cause. This Washington did with a polish that impressed even hostile Englishmen like Howe, not to mention a sympathetic Englishman such as Chatham, who informed the House of Lords (in February 1777), "America . . . is not a wild and lawless banditti, who having nothing to lose, might hope to snatch something from public convulsions; many of their leaders . . . have a great stake in this great contest: — *the gentleman who conducts their armies, I am told, has an estate of four or five thousand pounds a year.*[8] Even more important was the impression that Washington made upon the French. Perhaps he laid himself out to please them; if so, he succeeded to an astonishing degree. To nearly all he was a veritable Chevalier Bayard, *sans peur et sans reproche.* Here, they agreed, was a gentleman of quite unusual poise and integrity. What they say gains added force from the fact that, initially, France was prepared to urge the replacement of Washington by the Comte de Broglie, a Frenchman, as joint commander in chief. When de Kalb and other French-speaking observers had taken his measure, the notion was discarded.

Next, Congress wanted a commander who could raise and direct an army on the European model, fit to encounter professionals — a genuine Continental army, worthy of the United States. This was Washington's own overriding passion: to procure "Order, Regularity and Discipline." True, he thought mainly in terms of infantry, somewhat to the neglect of cavalry and other arms. But he envisioned an army of veterans; that is the essential fact — and the cause of much of his distress during the war years.

For, thirdly, Congress also wanted a commander whose forces would consist largely of short-service militiamen, irregulars — even, despite what Chatham said, "banditti." Congress wanted a man who could control such makeshift troops and exploit their special qualities. Here, perhaps, Congress began to expect too much of Washington. By temperament, at any rate, he was a shade too "European" for the circumstances of his America. His own experiences with militia, since Virginia frontier days, had been almost invariably unpleasant. It so happened that he was not present at any of the engagements — from Bunker, or Breed's, Hill to Cowpens — in which militia distinguished themselves. He was therefore reluctant to admit that militia had any virtues.[8] He had enough of confusion; he was not interested, except incidentally, in harassing the redcoats, but in beating them soundly by pitched battle. Yet even there he did as much as Congress was entitled to expect of any fallible mortal. Washington was certainly not a martinet, seeking blindly to impose an alien pattern of military etiquette upon Americans. He was well aware that American conditions

---

[8] At least, not unless properly trained and mustered. Some years later, when Washington attempted to secure a satisfactory military organization for the United States, he recognized that the regular army was bound to be a miniscule affair. He therefore recommended a well-trained militia as the basis of national defense. He never lived to see such a phenomenon, nor did generations of his successors, though they maintained the idea as a pious hope.

called for special and rather unorthodox military solutions. But he dreaded carrying the process too far. In style of generalship he closely resembled Cornwallis, and Cornwallis was a regular who liked to get a move on, with a well-trained army. That was also Washington's aim.

Wealthy gentleman, impeccable generalissimo, guerrilla warrior: Congress sought all these in the person of George Washington. In addition, Congress required such a paragon to think as a civilian. This putative commander, a dignified brigand capable of imposing his authority over forces, regular and militia, from thirteen different and semiautonomous states, must yet submit cheerfully to the supreme authority of Congress.

The marvel is that, demanding the impossible, Congress so nearly got it in George Washington. As a bonus, they found in him a man of quite extraordinary persistence. Fitzpatrick's huge edition of Washington's writings is unlikely to be read by many in its entirety. There are some ten thousand pages for the war years alone, and the documents in them are too minutely detailed and far too repetitive to whet one's appetite. Yet the repetition is vital to an understanding of the nature of the man. We watch him hammering away, in plain, workman-like prose, neither witty nor pompous, neither blustering nor apologetic, until he either gets his way or concludes that he has come to an absolute impasse. Particularly is this true when he writes of the means, however remote, of bringing the war to a close. Victory was the goal he kept in sight; unlike the British commanders, he never hopelessly confused the secondary advantage with the primary aim. Grand strategy was not his forte (and, perhaps he believed, not his business but that of Congress); after the failure of the Canada invasion in 1775-1776 he did not encourage ambitious projects of that kind. Instead, he concentrated upon what *must* be: a larger army, better ways of maintaining it, more prompt and more generous contributions from the states, the support of a navy that could, at lest for a space, wrest naval supremacy from the British. His long-deferred reward came at Yorktown.

David Ramsay of South Carolina, who published a *History of the American Revolution* in 1789, said, "It seemed as if the war not only required, but created talents." The remark well fits George Washington. He was never the "little paltry Colonel of Militia" that Lord Howe's secretary, Ambrose Serle, sneered at in 1776. His critics in America argued that he had not so much grown in stature as in public esteem. Yet even they, by the end of the war, had to admit that he wore his honors becomingly — and unassumingly. We can trace the process by working through those ten thousand crowded pages of his wartime writings. In them, little by little, we can detect the signs of greater assurance, wisdom and equanimity. The comments of French officers who met him in the later stages of the conflict (when he had mellowed a good deal) tell the same story. They speak of a man respected by nearly all, revered by some; capable of geniality if not of gaiety; keeping a good table but not a sot; well mounted and well-tailored but not a dandy; proud but not vainglorious – "His Excellency" in fact as well as in title.

His was not the only American talent created by the emergency. His reputation may have been unduly exalted at the expense of men like Horatio Gates. It could be argued that, placed in his shoes, others might have met the test as adequately. Philip Schuyler might have overcome his patrician manner, his New York parochialism, just as Washington learned to overcome certain Virginia prejudices against New England and other areas. Nathanael Greene, the Rhode Island Quaker general who fought so faithfully, might have satisfied his countrymen as supreme commander. It is hard to believe that the intelligent but morose and cynical Charles Lee could have stayed the course. But possibly Artemas Ward, whom Lee dismissed contemptuously as a "church warden," had talents for leadership that he never revealed after he felt shouldered aside in 1775. It is even conceivable that Benedict Arnold, given the glory he craved, would have burned away the resentments that instead made him a traitor. These are only conjectures. The sure and staggering truth is that Congress (and America) was luckier than it could reasonably hope to be in choosing Colonel Washington. The "available" man proved to be, despite all his minor defects, the indispensable man.

CHAPTER FOUR

PRESIDENT WASHINGTON

Farmer Washington – may he like a second Cincinnatus, be
called from the plow to rule a great people.

Toast offered at a Fourth of July celebration,
Wilmington, Delaware, 1788

"RETIRING WITHIN MYSELF"

General Washington longed to turn himself back into Farmer
Washington. He was physically and spiritually weary. His health was
indifferent – he had had a good deal of trouble with his teeth – and he
drooped under the cumulative weight of almost nine years of
responsibility. In fact, as he was soon to realize, Washington after 1783
was a private citizen who could never again enjoy true privacy. But it was
only natural that he should cherish a little, wistful dream of peace, that
he should conceive a rural idyll which we might call a kind of poetry.

The idyll was quickly overlaid by circumstance. Yet we can still trace it in the letters he wrote during the early months of 1784. This proud Virginia planter referred then to Mount Vernon, with a curious humbleness, as his "cottage" and his "villa" – words he had never used before in describing his domain. He saw himself as "a private citizen of America, on the banks of the Patowmac . . . under my own Vine and my own Fig-tree, free from the bustle of a camp and the intrigues of a court," who would henceforward "glide gently down the stream of life" until he was finally laid to rest. "I am not only retired from all public employments," he said, "but I am retiring within myself."

Perhaps he was half consciously playing the part of Cincinnatus. Plenty of people were comparing him to that patriot and making him sound more like a simple husbandman than an important landowner. But for a little while, at any rate, he was able to indulge the dream. He had ordered a quantity of books, in anticipation of ample leisure. (Some were travel narratives; they hint at a second dream, also to prove illusory, of a voyage to France, where Lafayette and others promised a warm welcome.) He resigned as vestryman of Truro Parish, without specifying his reason; possibly the post seemed to him one more minor "public employment" of which to rid himself. He made no attempt to enter into the political life of Virginia, though he could have had a seat in the state legislature more or less for the asking, or even the governorship. He held only one high office, in an honorary capacity: he was president-general of the Society of the Cincinnati, a commemorative organization of former army officers. But he had not been among the founders of the society, nor had he sought the distinction of heading it. Washington's hope was that he might, in the years to come, manage merely his own affairs.

These affairs, though, were exacting and various enough to dispel any lingering notion of a relaxed, secluded life. Three old enthusiasms soon engrossed him. The first, his particular pride, was his Mount Vernon home. The second was the practice of agriculture. The third was the development of Western lands. The three spread out in concentric circles of activity, until nothing was left of the brief vision of postwar placidity.

Mount Vernon could with fair accuracy have been called a cottage back in 1757, when Washington first began to improve the property. But by 1783 it was – according to American standards – a mansion, a great estate. Today, tourists see it as immaculate and serenely complete. In Washington's eyes, as he beheld Mount Vernon after years of exile, it was a half-finished sketch. While he might speak in metaphor of his vine and fig tree, he could not (so to speak) sit under them until they had been planted and coaxed into growth. So, within a month of his return

Washington was deep in correspondence on the state of the chimneys, paving for the piazza, suitable decorations for his "new room" or "banquet hall." From then on, his letters and his diary (which he had almost abandoned during the war) are crowded with detailed evidence of the care he lavished on Mount Vernon. He "purchased" indentured servants, newly arrived from Germany, to work as joiners and bricklayers. Inside the house, he concerned himself with wallpapers, bookshelves and Venetian blinds. Outside, he built an ambitious greenhouse; laid out roads, walks, lawns and shrubberies; redesigned his icehouse; fenced and stocked a deer park; constructed a fruit garden . . .

Beyond the house and its grounds lay the five Mount Vernon "farms," or "plantations" (either word will do – Washington used both – for he did not raise cotton but wheat, a "farm" crop; on the other hand, his workers were "plantation" slaves – some two hundred in all, including children and old folk). Since Washington came home with "empty hands" and was almost without ready cash, it was urgently necessary to set his affairs in order. Pride made him reject tentative proposals that he should, as America's First Citizen, receive a special allowance from Congress. Prudence insisted that he devote himself wholeheartedly to farming; so did inclination. In this respect he and Thomas Jefferson spoke the same language; a matter-of-fact vocabulary of seeds, manures and implements that fails to disguise their common underlying passion for what Washington called "the most delectable" of livelihoods. It was a laborious occupation, full of disappointment, yet there seems no doubt that Washington loved it. He sought advice from the English agriculturist Arthur Young, erected a barn to the latter's specification and imported an English farmer to superintend operations. He bred new strains of livestock, experimented with novel crops and systems of rotation and struggled to prevent soil erosion.

Washington's attention was not confined to Mount Vernon. His western tracts had yielded little or no profit; some were occupied by squatters or by farmers who disputed his title to them. In the autumn of 1784 he therefore set out once more across the Alleghenies, by the old route that held so many memories, to see for himself what was happening. But he got little satisfaction from the occupiers of his Virginia bounty lands, and was unable to journey farther and inspect his claims on the Ohio and Great Kanawha. Though the trip was to have important consequences, within the immediate context of his life it meant mainly a break in an unending round of duties at Mount Vernon. Washington could not find a secretary until the summer of 1785, with the result that (as he grumbled to a friend):

> I can with truth assure you, that at no period of the war have I been obliged to write half as much as I now do. . . . What with letters (often of an unmeaning nature) from foreigners, Enquiries after Dick, Tom, and Harry who *may have been* in some part, or at *sometime*, in the Continental service. Letters or certificates of service for those who want to go out of their own State. Introductions; applications for copies of Papers; references of a thousand old matters with which I *ought* not to be troubled, more than the Great Mogul; but which must receive answer of some kind, deprive me of my usual exercise; and without relief, may be injurious to me as I already begin to feel the weight, and oppression of it in my head.

People asked him for loans. Friends and neighbors sought his opinion. His own conscience impelled him to watch over the doings – not always wise or successful doings – of his many relatives.

The Cincinnati added to Washington's burden. No sooner was the society instituted then, to the dismay of its president-general, an outcry arose in several states. Its members saw the society as a harmless association of veterans, who in naming it after Cincinnatus had deliberately emphasized their peaceful intentions. Its enemies thought it at best a comically snobbish club (membership was hereditary, and confined to officers) and at worst an inner council of would-be aristocrats. Washington did his best to meet these objections, but the society continued to cause him embarrassment.

And although he enjoyed company, his appetite was surfeited at Mount Vernon. The man and his home had become a port of call for visitors of every sort, from old acquaintances to inquisitive foreigners. They filled his guest rooms week after week, winter and summer, eating up his provisions by the ton and drinking his wine by the gallon. Thus, one night in 1785, Washington, his family, and several guests had already gone to bed when they were aroused by the arrival of the French sculptor Houdon, who had come to do a portrait of Washington. Room was found somehow for Houdon and his three assistants. While they were his guests, Washington was having part of the roof shingled, and there was a wedding at the house between Washington's nephew and namesake George Augustine (who replaced Lund Washington as estate manager), and Martha Washington's niece, Frances Bassett. Not until June 1785 could the besieged proprietor of Mount Vernon note in his diary, "Dined with only Mrs. Washington, which I believe is the first instance of it since my retirement from public life." Such isolation remained a rarity.

All in all, however, the George Washington of these years was probably as happy as he had ever been. If correspondence was a nuisance, it must have gratified him to receive tributes from all over the world. The King of Spain presented him with a jackass (the broad humor of this was not lost on Washington, who named the animal Royal Gift and joked about its sluggish performance at stud); an English admirer gave him a marble fireplace; a Frenchman sent a pack of hounds; a European nobleman requested a portrait of Washington for inclusion in a gallery of military heroes. Remembering (if he did) his own abortive collection of that kind, Washington was entitled to feel that the Virginia colonel of militia was at last reaping his reward.

There were other compensations. Little by little, he established a routine that enabled him, without slighting his guests, to handle his own affairs. For exercise there was the almost daily ride around his farms, and in the winter months the delight of fox hunting. There was the pleasure of watching Mount Vernon approach the elegance he had planned for it; the comfort of a congenial marriage (though visitors occasionally found the General disagreeably stiff, they all praised Martha's amiable temper); and the stimulation of young children – two of Jackie Custis's offspring were adopted by the Washingtons after their mother remarried.

Above all, there was his third enthusiasm, for opening up the country. In 1782 he had taken advantage of a quiet spell to travel in northern New York and buy a tract there. He was still interested in the Dismal Swamp, between Virginia and North Carolina. And there were exciting prospects somewhat nearer home. Indeed, one of the purposes of his western journey in 1784 was to examine these. He came back convinced that Virginia and the West could and should be linked by water. The Potomac was navigable for a considerable distance upstream, and only a short portage divided it from the headwaters of the Ohio River system. When the necessary improvements had been made (the chief one a canal around the Potomac falls), he pictured a vigorous, ever-growing traffic that would flow along this new highway past his own front door. The effect (which he set out in a long diary entry that reads like the first draft of a prospectus) would be to increase trade, to hasten the settlement of the back country (with profit, of course, to the owners of trans-Allegheny lands) and – last but not least – to bind the men of the interior to the Union. Otherwise, already restless, they might fall victim to the wiles of Spain and Britain, which were in control of the Mississippi and Great Lakes exits from the Ohio valley.

The more Washington pondered the scheme the more it appealed. Without realizing quite where his boldness would eventually lead him, Washington began to set events in motion. Such schemes were being widely discussed in the central states; a James River route was also in fashion. Since Virginia shared rights to the Potomac with Maryland, local jealousies might result in deadlock. But, acting swiftly and helped by the prestige of his name, Washington secured the approval of both state legislatures in the winter of 1784-1785. As a commissioner for Virginia, he met with representatives from Maryland; and a Potomac River Company came into being, with himself as its (reluctant) president, under the patronage of the two states, which both guaranteed support. A James River Company was also created.

The Potomac commissioners ratified their joint agreement at Mount Vernon in the spring of 1785. A suggestion that Maryland and Virginia should meet annually in the future was generally welcomed. Gradually the idea grew in scope, until in January 1786 the Virginia legislature issued an invitation to all states of the Union to confer with its own commissioners and review matters of common interest concerning trade and commerce. Out of the proposal came the Annapolis convention of September 1786, to which five states (including Virginia) sent representatives. One of the Virginia delegates, James Madison, recommended in a report that another convention should be held in May 1787, at Philadelphia. Out of this, as everyone knows, came the new Constitution. The new Constitution provided for a President of the United States. The new President was George Washington.

TOWARD A NEW CONSTITUTION

Some of Washington's more eulogistic biographers have made his career practically synonymous with American history as a whole during his lifetime, placing him in the center of the stage at every episode. Tracing his story backward, they have seen a direct causal chain of circumstances all the way from his mission to Fort Le Boeuf in 1753 to his statesmanlike plan for the Potomac Company and thence, step by logical step, to the full glory of the Presidency in 1789. See, they proclaim, Washington *is* the Father of His Country; with uncanny prescience and a perfect sense of the true meaning of the Union he guides events, from early manhood to righteous old age.

Now this contention is not entirely wrong. We *can* discern an oddly circumstantial sequence; Washington *does* have a knack of being on hand at the place and moment where history is being made. But, before the

Revolutionary War, there is an element of accident in the pattern. In those days he achieved a measure of distinction, but he did not (in the eyes of his contemporaries, at any rate) achieve true greatness. That he accomplished in the war itself. In retirement afterwards, he was a factor in the national scene; whatever he did tended to have national repercussions, and whatever he did not do was also, negatively, a factor of national importance. Washington was well aware of this; and even if he had not been, his experience as president-general of the Cincinnati was well calculated to ram home the lesson.

The problem in considering Washington's development between 1783 and 1789 is this: did he achieve further greatness in his own right, or was further greatness thrust upon him, as something he could not avoid? Did he take a lead in re-forming the Union, or was he merely brought in, so to speak, in an honorary capacity? Or does the truth lie somewhere between such extremes? And behind this problem is another one, which still engages historians in vehement debate: what was the actual state of the Union during the years of the Confederation? Was this "the critical period," or was America in fact flourishing? Did the United States really *need* a new instrument of government? And (to come back to our hero) did Washington himself genuinely believe that the Union was in danger? If so, did he make up his own mind, or did others plant the notion?

Perhaps no final answers to such questions are possible. But they are worth raising, to shake our minds free of the conventional, oversimplified picture of George Washington – even if we end up with explanations not wildly dissimilar to the usual ones.

Temperamentally and from his experience as commander in chief, Washington favored a strong national government – or at least one that would be more effectual in moments of emergency than the wartime Congress he had served. This is clear from his Circular to the States, a lengthy memorandum compiled in June 1783, which is condensed to a phrase in the toast he offered at a dinner in Philadelphia, the day before he surrendered his commission: "Competent powers to Congress for general purposes." There is an implication (which, because of his scrupulous modesty, appears only now and then in his letters) that *he* had begun the work, and through example and precept had indicated the path for the new nation to follow. Thus, in a letter to John Jay (Foreign Secretary under the Confederation) Washington speaks a little pontifically of the way in which his fellow countrymen have neglected his "sentiments and opinions . . . tho' given as a last legacy in the most solumn manner." To this extent did he identify himself with America:

his own reputation and hers were inextricably interwoven, and it hurt him that America should present to outsiders a spectacle of disunity. He was especially sensitive to British reactions, and naturally annoyed that the British – the enemy he had beaten – refused to evacuate various Western posts according to their treaty obligations. It was the more galling that the British had some excuse, since several American states had likewise failed to honor their treaty promises.

But the letter to Jay was sent in the summer of 1786 and does not accurately convey Washington's outlook in the previous couple of years. At that period he shrank from involvement. Cato or Cincinnatus, he had played his part and said his piece. He was now a bystander, determined to devote his remaining years to the consolidation of his private fortunes. Though he had no direct heirs, that did not lessen his zeal to have and to hold like any other Virginia dynast. True, he had a sharper sense than most of America's nationhood, real and potential. But it should be noted that the Potomac plan aroused his pride *as a Virginian.* The plan was recommended to him by another Virginian, Jefferson; and after he had assumed control, Washington initially thought in regional rather than national terms. Writing to Northern acquaintances, he stressed the urgency of thwarting Britain; to men of his own area, he disclosed that he was equally concerned with the rivalry of the "Yorkers" and their route to the interior via the Hudson.

This is not to say that Washington behaved dishonestly, but only that in 1784-1785 he was not thinking in grandly Continental terms. His state pride never ran counter to the interests of America as a whole. Yet for a spell these interests receded: they did not dominate his imagination. Friends in Congress kept in touch with him; his bulging post bag brought news of conditions in most parts of the Union, from Massachusetts to Georgia. But Congress was a long way off, shifting, as it did, away from Annapolis to Trenton, and then further, to New York. Domestically absorbed, anxious to maintain the proprieties of retirement, uncertain as to the true import of what his correspondents told him, sick of dissension, Washington expressed his opinions with oracular vagueness. It was men like John Jay, Henry Lee and James Madison who committed themselves (though also warily), who took the lead in the move for a new government. They wanted to enlist his aid not for his pen or his brain but for his name. To Americans, Washington was victory, rectitude – and, for the moment, something of a cipher. Surely, Jay told him in March 1786, he could not watch the disintegration of America "with the eye of an unconcerned spectator"? Sounding him out, Jay went on: "An opinion begins to prevail, that a

General Convention for revising the articles of Confederation would be expedient." Replying, a month later, Washington agreed broadly that the "fabrick" was "tottering"; but he confined himself to cautious generalities.

Again, this is not to accuse Washington of stupidity or irresponsibility, but merely to emphasize that he had no ready solution to offer. Viewed as an agglomeration of farmers and merchants, America was prospering. Congress was not entirely inept; it was the legitimate government of the land. If Congress were not willing to reform itself, could reform be legally imposed by some *ad hoc* convention? What would people say? What would the states say? On the other hand, the Articles of Confederation, in practice, did not admit of firm national government; the states were dangerously indifferent to Congress and antagonistic to one another. *Something* should be done.

Following some way behind the active controversialists, as he had done before 1775, Washington gradually began to sort out his ideas. Thus on August 1, 1786, he wrote three letters. Two went to France, to the Chevalier de la Luzerne and the American minister, Thomas Jefferson. The third was to Jay in New York. The first two were cheerful in tone, the third full of foreboding. Why the discrepancy? In large part because Washington did not wish to discredit America's reputation abroad; even to his bosom friend Lafayette he spoke of America with a perhaps forced optimism. In art, too, because he was divided in his mind, and so reacted differently to different correspondents. So, he frankly acknowledged to the pessimistic Jay, "I cannot feel myself an unconcerned spectator. . . . Your sentiments, that our affairs are drawing rapidly to a crisis, accord with my own."

For Washington, the crisis revealed itself in the shape of Shay's Rebellion in Massachusetts, in the autumn of 1786. It was an abortive and incoherent rising of back-country malcontents. But both the rebellion and the way in which it was handled seemed to Washington symptomatic of profound disorder. Expletives were rare in his letters; now he burst out in alarm: *Are your people getting mad? . . . What is the cause of all this? When and how is it to end? . . .* These disturbances – *Good God! who besides a tory could have foreseen, or a Briton predicted them? . . . What, gracious God, is man! That there should be such inconsistency and perfidiousness in his conduct? . . . We are fast verging to anarchy and confusion!*

What should he do? For months he worried and hesitated, while more actively engaged Americans laid the groundwork for the Philadelphia convention of May 1787. Would he attend as a Virginia delegate? He was urged to declare himself. One uneasiness was removed early in 1787 when Congress gave the convention its blessing. But Washington was plagued by doubts. He was fifty-five, and felt older, racked with rheumatism, short of funds. He had already declined to attend the triennial meeting of the Cincinnati, which was also to be held in Philadelphia at the same time as the convention; how could he now disclose that his reasons for nonattendance were mere excuses? Above all, Washington shrank from associating himself with a body that might prove as impotent as the Annapolis convention of September 1786. If the northeastern states again held aloof, as they had done at Annapolis, the Philadelphia delegates would get nothing done. Worse, they might do harm – to the country and to their own reputations. Washington wanted no part in a conspiracy *or* a farce.

Douglas Southall Freeman, Washington's foremost biographer, thinks that his conduct at this period was unpleasantly egocentric. If America was in peril, Freeman wonders, why did he not rush to the rescue? This seems too harsh a verdict. The most that we can say of Washington is that he was, after all, a human being and not a sort of ideal permanent patriot-without-portfolio. His motives were not heroic, but they were understandable. Still, one wonders; can excessive modesty become almost the same thing as its opposite – inordinate vanity? Did it in his case?

Perhaps. The essential fact is that Washington did finally decide to go to Philadelphia. He arrived there in early May, was elected president of the convention by the unanimous wish of the other delegates, and sat in his chair of office through exhausting weeks of argument and maneuver, until the business was concluded in mid-September. There was one lengthy adjournment in August. Washington took advantage of it to visit his old encampment at Valley Forge and the town of Trenton, where he had caught the Hessians unaware. No doubt the interlude refreshed him; one would like to affirm that the glimpse of the past also moved him, but if so, he nevertheless wrote of other things in his diary.

His role in the Philadelphia convention, as it toiled through the hot summer, exactly suited him. Whenever a point was put to the vote, he appears to have stepped down from his chair to record his preference among the other delegates. Otherwise, he was able to maintain a certain detachment. As he listened, contributing little to the intricate sequence of debate, he could make up his mind at leisure, *in* and yet not exactly *of* the company, arbiter rather than advocate. Only one other man, Benjamin Franklin (who was also present), could have filled the presidential chair with equal appropriateness; but Franklin was past eighty and sick, though still not moribund.

Sometimes Washington voted on the losing side, and usually on what was to be known as the Federalist side; that is, for a strong national government and an effective executive within the government. Little by little, however, the Federalists carried the day. None of the delegates – including Washington – was entirely satisfied with the document that gradually emerged. A number were so disgusted that they withdrew from Philadelphia or would not put their signatures to the finished work. Some regretted the explicit surrender of provincial powers to the federal government. Those from such large states as Virginia and Massachusetts feared the loss of privileges not merely to the federal government, but to such smaller states as Delaware and New Jersey; and men from the smaller states clung to the principle of equal representation that had been granted under the Articles of Confederation. Several times the convention was near deadlock. But by degrees it moved forward; and Washington shared the conviction of a majority of his colleagues that its compromises were workmanlike. Politics was the art of the possible; the new Constitution was the best that could be drawn up in the circumstances.

Washington, at any rate, thought so. He could approve of its provisions for an executive (in the shape of a President), for a Congress (of two houses, a Senate and a House of Representatives) and for a judicial system headed by a federal Supreme Court. Each branch was separated from the others. The arrangement made sense to him in terms of his own experience; the President would be something like the Governor of Virginia (except that there would be no instructions and vetoes emanating from London), the Senate like the Governor's Council (with two members from each state, it would be a compact group of twenty-six seasoned counselors) and the House of Representatives comparable to the Virginia General Assembly. Indeed, Virginia would have an influential voice in its proceedings, since she as the most populous state would have more members – ten, for example, as against only one for lowly Rhode Island – than any other.

While the individual states would retain a degree of autonomy, the Constitution pleased Washington by putting teeth into the federal government. It would be able to present a united front to foreigners, to collect its revenues, to regulate its finances, and in general to ease the way for every law-abiding American, be he planter, farmer, manufacturer or merchant.

Washington could ride home in his coach to Mount Vernon that September with the conviction that he had done his duty. His own house was almost finished; as a final touch, an ironwork dove of peace was being added to Mount Vernon's cupola as a weathervane. But the new Constitution was still unfinished until it had been ratified by state conventions and put into effect. Washington's life entered a new phase, with almost as much distress and uncertainty as in the months before he set out for Philadelphia. He was committed to support the Constitution, and did what he could. Certainly in his own Virginia his influence helped to tip the balance. But he was disturbed by the protests in state after state The delegates at Philadelphia were accused (with some justice) of having exceeded their instructions. They had met in secret, not allowing their decisions to be announced until the end. They were intriguers, aristocrats. They were in too much of a hurry; let there be another convention to review the proposals of the first one. Such were some of the arguments against the Constitution makers. Radical Rhode Island had not even sent delegates to Philadelphia, and ratification seemed uncertain in several other states. It was not only debtors and paper-money men who attacked the Founding Fathers (or were they the Foundering Fathers?). There was enmity from disgruntled men of substance: Governor Clinton in New York, Governor John Hancock in Massachusetts, and – in Washington's own state – Patrick Henry, Richard Henry Lee, Edmund Randolph, even his old friend and neighbor George Mason.

Nine out of thirteen states had to approve the Constitution for it to be adopted. By January 1788 five states had ratified. In February Massachusetts came in by a narrow margin, swayed by the Federalist intimation to Hancock that he might be Vice-President, or even (if Virginia failed to ratify and Washington was thereby excluded) President under the new government. Hancock was won over. What was more, he introduced a valuable formula that was followed by other states: Massachusetts would accept the Constitution on the understanding that amendments would subsequently be adopted that would meet the criticisms raised against the document. These would amount to a Bill of Rights, similar to the provisions already incorporated in various state constitutions.

Two more states came in, making a total of eight; and Virginia, the most crucial of all, came in at the end of June after a tense struggle. Better still, it was learned in Virginia that New Hampshire had already ratified. Ten states were in, one more than the necessary minimum. Alexander Hamilton and other ardent Federalists in New York used the glad news to disarm opposition in that state. A year after the delegates dispersed from Philadelphia, the Constitution they had drawn up was sanctioned, with or without reservations, by eleven out of thirteen states.

Only North Carolina and Rhode Island stood outside. Their obstinacy, though unfortunate, was not fatal.

What next? For the nation as a whole, it remained for Congress to wind itself up and for a new Congress to be chosen. There was a squabble over the seat of the future government, ending in the tentative agreement that it should remain temporarily at New York. For Washington, there was the virtual certainty that he would be elected President. His name had been freely used by Federalists in the debates over ratification. Someone had suggested that the Federalists should be known "by the name of Washingtonians," and that the Anti-Federalists should be named Shaysites after Daniel Shays, the Massachusetts rebel. Once the terms of the Constitution were published, Washington seemed the obvious candidate for the Presidency. Only he was known, respected and trusted in all the states. Only he, apart from the aged Franklin, had the requisite magic, glory, prestige (there is no adequate word for this quality) demanded of those who are to fill the great offices of government. So the newspapers told him; so his friends insisted. "In the name of America, of mankind at large, and your own fame," Lafayette wrote in January 1788, "I beseech you, my dear General, not to deny your acceptance of the office of President for the first years. You only can settle that political machine."

Washington's own emotions were mixed. He was gratified, embarrassed and alarmed. The honor proposed was immense. But how could he discuss it until it became actual? A foregone conclusion was not quite the same thing as an election. If he were offered the Presidency, he must accept. But if he accepted, how could he endure four more years of the strain of life in the pitiless limelight? No one else was better prepared, certainly, to undertake the task. But was he himself well enough prepared?" "I should," he said, "consider myself as entering upon an unexplored field, enveloped on every side with clouds and darkness." However, at the time that he wrote thus, in the autumn of 1788, it was taken for granted by his acquaintances that he would be President. All through the winter they reminded him briskly of his duty, while he without enthusiasm thought of his coming trial. In April 1789, waiting at Mount Vernon for the news that was bound to come, Washington told his old friend Henry Knox, in confidence:

> My movements to the chair of Government will be accompanied by feelings not unlike those of a culprit who is going to the place of his execution: so unwilling am I, in the evening of a life nearly consumed in public cares, to

quit a peaceful abode for an Ocean of difficulties, without
that competency of political skill, abilities and inclination
which is necessary to manage the Helm. I am sensible, that
I am embarking the voice of my Countrymen and a good
name of my own, on this voyage, but what returns will be
made for them, Heaven alone can foretell.

FIRST ADMINISTRATION: 1789-1793

A fortnight later the suspense, though not the apprehension, was
over. Washington had received every vote in the electoral college,
Congress informed him; and John Adams of Massachusetts had got
enough votes to qualify as his Vice-President. Washington set out at
once for New York. All along the road – a muddy road that took eight
days to travel – he met with a tumultuous reception: flowers, banners,
triumphal arches, addresses of welcome, militia escorts, extravagant
newspaper tributes to "our adored leader and ruler."

To the beholder he was a magnificent figure. Inwardly, he was full
of dread. His popularity could not be doubted in face of such lavish
proofs. But each fresh demonstration deepened his anxiety; his
countrymen, in praising him as superhuman, would also make
superhuman demands upon him. How correspondingly terrible would
his crash be, if he failed in a task that he could not even adequately
define to himself! Thirteen disparate states, two of them still outside the
Union of a Constitution that was still in the hazard, all jealous for their
"darling sovereignty," stretching up the Atlantic seaboard for fifteen
hundred miles; a population of less than four million (the exact figure
was unknown), of whom nearly one in five were Negro slaves; a nation
new to nationality, undertaking the experiment of federal republicanism,
burdened by debt, menaced by external enemies – what might happen if
the worst should come to the worst?

However, it must be counted among Washington's major virtues
that he never lost his nerve. In some men, anxiety causes a general
paralysis of the will or onsets of sudden directionless energy. In
Washington it induced a certain extra caution, but also an extra, dogged
adherence to the job in hand.

A sour critic at the time – and there were one or two whose
skepticism touched even the majestic figure of Washington in 1789 –
could feel that at this tremendous moment in America's history the
Chief Executive did not quite fulfill expectations. Bothered by private
matters – his debts, the proper care of Mount Vernon during his absence,

the furnishing of his house in New York, points of protocol, the need to vindicate himself against the charge (which no one was making) that he had been false to his previous pledges of retirement – all these made him appear a trifle wooden. At least, they did in the eyes of such a witness as William Maclay, a caustic and irreverent senator from Pennsylvania. Half awed and half derisive, Maclay noted of Washington's inaugural address:

> This great man was agitated and embarrassed more than ever he was by the leveled cannon or pointed musket. He trembled, and several times could scarce make out to read, though it must be supposed he had often read it before.

His gestures were maladroit, Maclay said; and his costume could also have been thought odd, since Washington wore a worsted suit of American manufacture together with the dress sword and white silk stockings of European court ceremony. Nor was there anything particularly memorable in the actual text of his address. It was ponderous, official; satisfactory, but not overwhelming.

Yet, unlike Maclay, most of the crowd who saw Washington inaugurated that April day were deeply stirred. If he was a little awkward, they forgave him and even trusted him the more. Washington was to discover what he no doubt already suspected: that his unique standing in the nation was a priceless asset. Other elements were on his side. He was not an expert on finance, or a nimble political tactician, or a constitutional theorist, or a diplomatist acquainted at firsthand with foreign affairs. But as commander in chief and as president of the Constitutional Convention he had gained some familiarity with these and other aspects of government, not to mention what he had learned in earlier days at Williamsburg and elsewhere. Whatever he might lack in the higher arts of polity, he was an honest, canny and methodical administrator. Thus, he had been deluged with requests from men seeking appointments under the new government. With his usual blunt good sense he had refused to commit himself to any of them. He came to New York with a heavy heart but with clean hands.

Fortunately, no immediate crisis threatened in the summer of 1789. Congress was slow to assemble and occupied itself for a while mainly with minor problems of procedure and so on. All was not sweetness and light in Congress. The prolonged squabbles over the site for the permanent seat of the federal government revealed that sectional jealousies were still very much alive; and there were signs of more fundamental dissension. Even so, Congress and the nation as a whole accepted the new Constitution with remarkably little fuss. The necessary amendments to form a Bill of Rights were drawn up, submitted to the states and ratified without much trouble. North Carolina and Rhode Island thereupon both entered the Union. A Judiciary Act, to fill out the constitutional provision for a federal court system, was also passed in 1789. Within a few months of Washington's inauguration, the document conceived at Philadelphia was taking on a life of its own. It was being accepted without demur as the given frame of reference. Indeed, while Washington was venerated as one symbol of American union, the Constitution was likewise assuming an almost sacred character as a second and more permanent symbol of that union. Much as Americans respected George Washington, even more did they respect the notion of representative government. They interpreted the notion in different ways. The debates in Congress were rancorous at times and petty at others. But they were carried on within the frame of reference – the parliamentary frame, in which Americans were at home through long experience. The Constitution was workable because a majority of Americans wished it to work. Without that vital element of habitual skill and harmony, all of Washington's labors and exhortations would have been in vain.

His way was made easier also in that the new government in 1789 inherited tangible features of the old one; there was a degree of continuity in actual institutions. The President benefited in personal terms by being able to add William Jackson, the former secretary of the Continental Congress, to his own small group of secretaries – Tobias Lear, David Humphreys and other knowledgeable, articulate men. More largely, he benefited from the survival of the old executive departments, some of whose heads had been closely associated with Washington in the past. Under the Constitution, the departments were mentioned only obliquely. But Congress passed the necessary legislation to renew them and, after some argument, conceded that the President should have the right – a crucial one – to remove his executive officers as well as to appoint them.

He retained Henry Knox of Massachusetts, his former artillery chief, as Secretary of War. John Jay of New York, who had been Secretary of Foreign Affairs since 1784, became the first Chief Justice of the Supreme Court. In Jay's place, at the head of the redesignated Department of State, Washington put his brilliant Virginia friend Thomas Jefferson. Another Virginian, Edmund Randolph (who had in the meantime overcome his scruples with regard to the Constitution), was given office as Attorney General. As for the Treasury, which ranked in importance with the State Department, this had recently been administered by a small committee. Washington, instead, entrusted it to one man, Alexander Hamilton of New York, who, though still in his early thirties, had already made his mark as soldier, lawyer and theorist. Finally, the postal organization that Benjamin Franklin had once directed was given to Postmaster General Samuel Osgood, a former member of the Treasury board. All prominent men, all more or less familiar with their new functions. Indeed, New York was thronged with men who had contributed to American independence and union in one way or another. James Madison, for example, though kept out of the Senate by opposition in Virginia, was a leading figure in the House of Representatives.

So far, Washington was merely implementing legislation contrived in Congress to amplify what was already sketched in the Constitution. Many matters were still left in doubt. Among these was the precise nature of the Presidency. Washington and his contemporaries were in broad agreement that the Chief Executive should, while sharing certain powers and duties with the two branches of Congress, nevertheless stand somewhat aloof. In the Constitutional Convention, Franklin spoke against a salary for the President, on the grounds that (as British politics dreadfully revealed) a "Post of Honour" that was also a "Place of Profit" was calculated to bring out the worst excesses of ambition and avarice. Washington had taken no salary, but merely his expenses, while commander in chief; and now in his inaugural address he proposed the same rule. He might well have ruined himself if the suggestion had been adopted. Happily for himself and his successors, Congress fixed the President's annual salary at $25,000. For 1789 it was a most substantial income, lifting him far above the Secretary of State and Treasury Secretary with their $3,500 apiece, or above members of Congress with their six dollars a day.

He was expected, then, to maintain a fairly high style. But (in the words of the old riddle) how high was high? There was no perfect answer. To live in splendor was to risk the hostility of men like Maclay, who were still suspicious that some Americans hankered after monarchy; to practice undue economy was to expose the Presidency to contempt. Washington's compromise pleased most of his countrymen. It was the compromise implicit in his inaugural costume, when he wore the apparel of a gentleman who was nevertheless unmistakably an American gentleman. Dignity and common sense were his guides. What should his title be? John Adams, presiding over the Senate, made himself a little ridiculous by insisting on kingly designations. "His Highness, the President of the United States of America, and Protector of their Liberties" was the formula suggested by the Senate. The House, however, wanted the plain title "President of the United States"; and Washington (though he is often said to have preferred "His Mightiness, the President of the United States") had the wisdom to let the argument die a natural death, until by general usage he was simply "Mr. President."

Common sense, too, determined his policy on entertaining and on public visits. At Mount Vernon he had kept open house. That was impossible in New York; so, taking advice beforehand, he established a system of weekly levees, at which formal calls could be paid, and of dinner parties (usually in the late afternoon, when the levee ended). He accepted no private invitations, though – indulging his fondness for plays – he frequently relaxed among guests at the theater. Taking advice again, he decided to travel in different parts of the Union. And again he sought a balance; if he toured New England in 1789, he paid his respects to the Southern states two years later.

Perhaps it was all a little on the stiff side. Certainly this could be said of his relations with Congress. Both were on their best behavior; and best behavior is not easy behavior. His addresses produced formal replies, which in turn brought forth replies to the replies. One result, unforeseen by the Founding Fathers, was that the President and the Senate drew apart. Perhaps it was inevitable, since all branches of the new government were so tensely aware of their own privileges and of the precedents that were being created at every step. But some coldness and bewilderment were caused. Instead of becoming his inner council, the Senate maintained its distance from Washington. Only once did he come to the Senate in person, to confer on foreign policy – an area in which the Executive and Senate were supposed to share responsibility. The occasion was dismally unsuccessful. If Maclay is to be believed, Washington was haughty and impatient, and departed irritably when the Senate was unwilling to give immediate assent to his wishes.

However, even Maclay admits that when Washington came back after the adjournment, he seemed perfectly good-humored. If he never repeated the experiment, neither did he persist in what might have been a disastrous relationship. In any case, Washington was not short of advice. During the first years his closest ties were with James Madison. Madison came to see him, prepared papers for him and gave constitutional opinions. When Washington planned to retire at the end of his first term, it was Madison who in 1792 wrote the initial draft of what was to emerge four years afterward as the celebrated Farewell Address. He leaned heavily, too, upon Alexander Hamilton and – somewhat less – upon John Jay and Vice-President Adams. Gradually he came to rely more and more on the heads of the executive departments. It was an unplanned process, for no one had envisaged the President as Prime Minister. Yet, in effect, by the end of Washington's first administration, he was equipped with a "cabinet." The word was in use, and the idea in embryonic being.

By then, also unplanned, Washington was confronted by something like a party system. Indeed, he was the center of acute antagonisms, so that – for example – he and Madison fell almost completely out of step with one another. Madison, in his prescient way, had realized that "the spirit of party and faction" was bound to exist in any civilized nation, and that the reconciliation of such interest groups would, inevitably, be among the tasks of Congress and the Chief Executive. Washington too had recognized, before he became President, that – in addition to the usual provincial rivalries – the country was seriously divided over the new Constitution. He thought it quite likely that the Anti-Federalists would vote against him in the electoral college.

Washington and many others with him were dismayed to find that the adoption of the Constitution focused argument rather than ended it. In general, those who had actively supported the Constitution in 1787-1788 were ranged against those who had had misgivings. They continued to call themselves Federalists and Anti-Federalists, and to quarrel noisily over the desired shape of their infant nation. There was no neat division. Some men, such as Madison and Randolph, changed their minds. Differences of opinion were met within the same family; Fisher Ames of Massachusetts, the Federalists' most eloquent champion in the House of Representatives, had no fiercer enemy than his own brother Nathaniel, who even refused to attend Fisher's funeral some years later – alleging that it was being staged as a piece of Federalist propaganda. Roughly, though, the Federalists (the "prigarchy," in Nathaniel Ames's view) were men of substance: merchants, lawyers and the like, Easterners, for the most part. Their opponents ("mobocrats," as against "monocrats," in the terminology of the time) were in opposition for various reasons. Some still disliked the idea of a strong national government, or even the principle of administrative authority. Government, for them as for Tom Paine, was "the lost badge of innocence." Others, especially in the West and South, objected to the Federalists as a clique of selfish businessmen.

The struggle that resulted was, for at least four reasons, intensely distasteful and disturbing to Washington. First, it pained him that the stability of the Union should be threatened at all. Second, the battle as fought within his own, executive branch of the government. Third, it extended to the field of foreign policy. Fourth, it directly involved his own reputation.

When Washington took office in 1789, he believed – not out of arrogance but because so many Americans had told him so – that he was needed at the helm. Or, if we must use a nautical metaphor, it is better to say that he was needed on the bridge. America's primary requirement, as he saw it, was confidence. *Crescit eundo* – She grows as she goes – could well have been the Union's official motto. In the words of his Farewell Address, "time and habit are at least as necessary to fix the true character of government as of other human institutions." Let the Union be set on the right lines and all else would follow. Let there be a small navy and army, and a suitable militia organization to keep the peace; let the revenues be collected, the laws obeyed, native pride encouraged; let things run in their own fashion thereafter. This was his philosophy. America and the Union were potentially sound, potentially great. It was not a doctrine that he expressed lyrically or analyzed with much subtlety. But he was not whistling to keep his spirits up. It was an article of faith, something that he *felt*.

This being so, Washington – as far as legislation was concerned – acted as Chief Magistrate rather than as Chief Executive. Alexander Hamilton, his Treasury Secretary, was much more positive. To Hamilton the Constitution was "a fabric which can hardly be stationary, and which will retrograde if it cannot be made to advance." It was, he argued, quoting Demosthenes, the duty of a statesman to "march at the head of affairs" and "produce the *event*." Confidence, then, was something to be contrived, nurtured – in fact, created. And by "a statesman" Hamilton meant himself.

Hamilton is one of the most fascinating figures in American history. If Washington puzzles us because he seems too good to be true, the mystery of Hamilton is by contrast that of an amazingly diverse and inconsistent personality. By turns devoted and self-seeking, meticulous and slovenly, shrewd and reckless, cynical and righteous, practical and visionary, he would have been a handful for any President in any period. At a time when the details of government were still unsettled, this supremely confident and extraordinarily able young man threatened to dominate the executive and to emerge as a kind of Prime Minister, with Washington as a kind of limited constitutional monarch.

Ambitions aside, Hamilton had some grounds for defining his

position thus. In contemporary Britain (whose affairs he studied closely and whose constitution he revered), William Pitt, even more youthful than Hamilton, was both Prime Minster and Chancellor of the Exchequer. Some regulation of American finances was in any case essential; Hamilton's plans were therefore bound to figure prominently in Washington's first administration. Moreover, Hamilton's appointment was worded so as to suggest that, among the executive heads, he might have a special function as an intermediary between President and Congress. Finally, the other chief executive head, Thomas Jefferson, did not take office until six months after Hamilton – six vital months during which Hamilton's advice was constantly sought on all major problems, including foreign policy, and unfailingly given.

The consequences were almost catastrophic, since Jefferson and Hamilton were soon at loggerheads. It is possible to overstress the Hamiltonian-Jeffersonian polarity as a fundamental division in the story of America. The ideological gulf between them was less extreme than that of many other episodes in history. Yet there is no denying the sharpness of their conflict or the tumult of American faction that they typified. As great a figure as Hamilton, perhaps even greater, Thomas Jefferson was less pugnacious. Unlike Hamilton, he hated to become personally involved in controversy and had little of Hamilton's passion to be at the top; the high dangerous places did not beckon him. Hamilton had led troops in battle (storming a redoubt at Yorktown) and was eager to risk his hand again (incidentally, he could not resist doing the Secretary of War's job, when he got the chance, as well as his own and the Secretary of State's). Jefferson had never been a soldier and made no pretense of martial quality.

Nevertheless, the two men clashed, angrily and often. Jefferson was well enough pleased with the Constitution, once the Bill of Rights was incorporated in it. But, in the eyes of Jefferson, Madison and many others, Hamilton's policies were ultra-Federalist, viciously so. These policies were sanctioned by Washington; most of them were adopted; and they now seem such commonplaces of America's heritage that it takes an imaginative effort to see why they stirred up so much protest.

The main reason is, of course, that Hamilton's proposals appealed strongly to the conservative and mercantile elements in the Union and were correspondingly antipathetic to other, radical and agrarian groups. It was difficult in the circumstances to arrive at any compromise; one set of interests or the other was bound to be dissatisfied. The initial problem, which Hamilton tackled in 1790, was that of America's debts. These, which had been incurred during the Revolutionary War, amounted to about eighty million dollars, of which twenty-five million were owed by individual states. Hamilton proposed to honor them in full, though the paper securities which represented the various debts were greatly depreciated. He proposed, that is, to fund the national debt at face value and to assume the state debts as a national liability, almost at par. Hamilton won the debate, basing his case on national honor and national confidence – both arguments that seemed sound to Washington. The arguments against funding and assumption were varied; but perhaps the most heated was that of Hamilton's scheme to enrich the speculator: the usual holder of paper securities was not the original owner, who had bought them for patriotic reasons and sold them through necessity at a discount, but the crafty Easterner who was thereby subsidized by the Federal Government. Hamilton himself was well aware of the process, but he saw its implications in a different light. His measures would (he rightly predicted) "cement" the Union by attaching to it every group that acquired a financial stake in its well-being.

As Hamilton's plans unfolded, Jefferson became the more enraged, because he had been persuaded to support funding and assumption – and bring his influence to bear in Congress – by a compromise that had nothing to do with finance. Hamilton, he felt, had tricked him in a piece of horse trading. By it, Hamilton's Northern friends in Congress voted with the Southerners on the vexed issue of the national capital. With these votes the South was able, so to speak, to pull the projected site down as far as the Potomac instead of merely to Philadelphia, where Congress was to move until 1800, when it was expected that the new "Federal City" would be ready for occupation. True, this was a concession to the South – and moreover, a source of quiet pleasure to Washington, whose home would be only a few miles away along the river. But it seemed an empty victory to set against Hamilton's Federalist molding of the Constitution.

Early in 1791 the Treasury Secretary and the Secretary of State clashed violently in front of the President. Hamilton wished to establish a national bank, under governmental auspices, and had reported so to the House of Representatives in one of his masterly documents. The measure aroused such an outcry that Washington asked his executive heads to submit their written opinions, not as to whether a national bank would be desirable but whether it would be constitutional. Hamilton naturally answered, again in masterly fashion, that it was. Jefferson, with equal brilliance, contended that the Constitution could not be stretched so far. What should Washington do? The two opinions were diametrically opposed. Neither seemed to him entirely tenable. Yet, since Congress had passed the bill, it remained to him only to sign or veto. As it was Hamilton's brain child, not Jefferson's, he decided to sign. Soon afterward he approved an excise bill that Hamilton had likewise recommended, in order to augment the separate revenues derived from import duties. The excise was to be levied on distilled liquor, which formed the main livelihood for many Western farmers. Hence another division of opinion.

Funding, assumption, a national bank, the excise tax: all seemed to Madison and Jefferson to prove that Hamilton was in power and would corrupt America if he continued to win. Gone would be the prospect of a tranquil land of enlightened agrarians. Instead, the "monocrats" would consolidate their hold and turn America into a plausible imitation of Europe. Congress would be packed with placemen; and if the poison spread, America would revert to hereditary dynastic rule. The remedy, if any, was to combat Hamilton. Jefferson was reluctant to take the lead; like Washington, he longed to be a private citizen again in his native Virginia. But events had a momentum of their own. Little by little, Jefferson, Madison and a few associates emerged as the spokesmen of those Americans who thought of themselves as Anti-Federalists. As their loose and somewhat accidental coalition became more self-aware, it adopted a new name: its members called themselves Democratic-Republicans, or Republicans for short.

One symptom of the growing rift was the establishment in October 1791 of a Republican paper, the *National Gazette.* While not the first newspaper to attack the Federalists, it was the first to offer an effective – in fact, a devastating – challenge at the national level of the Federalist *Gazette of the United States,* which had come into existence with the new government in 1789, under the editorship of John Fenno, and which unfailingly supported Hamilton. Fenno's rival editor, the poet Philip Freneau, was a college friend of Madison, and an ardent Republican. A much more enterprising journalist than Fenno, he was also employed as a part-time translator in the Department of State. Since Freneau was getting the better of the argument in 1792, Hamilton (writing for Fenno under a variety of pen names) accused the poet of being Jefferson's lackey. Freneau countered with equal ferocity.

To a later generation the situation may seem fantastic. Washington's two most important cabinet members are engaged, by clandestine means that deceived nobody, in a bitter and fundamental quarrel. The other executive heads were tending to take sides, Knox with Hamilton and Randolph with his fellow Virginian Jefferson. Hamilton was still actively (if secretly) concerning himself with foreign affairs. Nor were clear lines drawn in other directions. Hamilton took over the postmaster-general's organization, which would have been more suitably entrusted to the Department of State; and the new federal mint, which ought logically to have been put under the Treasury, was instead put under Jefferson. Was it all muddle and antagonism?

Not at the time, as Washington's age saw it. The "cabinet" had as yet little coherence; nor had the alignment of "parties." Only in a rough and undefined sense were the programs of the executive heads taken to be those of the President himself, still less of a unanimous Administration. Both Hamilton and Jefferson respected the President and believed they were loyal to him and to their different ideas of the Union. In his presence they did not squabble. Their grievances were directed at one another, not at Washington; and each, it must be said, admired the other while distrusting him. Though there was a feud, there was not a hopeless crisis. If Washington was a somewhat remote figure who did not actively devise and promote legislation, he was not a fool or a weakling. During his first term no one seriously accused him of being Hamilton's dupe. He had known Hamilton intimately for four years in the Revolutionary War, when Hamilton was an aide-de-camp. He had heard Hamilton's conservative views on government expressed at the Philadelphia convention in 1787. He had had ample opportunity to read what Freneau and others thought of Hamilton's "system." No doubt he was deeply impressed by the young man's intellectual ability. Perhaps he knew from wartime conversations with his aide that even as far back as 1776 Hamilton was already fascinated by problems of finance and trade. No doubt, also, he realized the flaws in Hamilton's temperament – a knowledge he must have gained at least as early as 1781, when Hamilton, after an imagined slight, withdrew from Washington's headquarters in a fit of pique.

Nevertheless, 1792 was an uneasy year for the President. Until the summer, he fully intended to retire from an office that he had not enjoyed. He had suffered two serious illnesses – a tumor on the thigh in 1789 and a bout of pneumonia in 1790; and in his letters we find several references to his weakening powers of memory. He was aging, and Mount Vernon seemed increasingly dear to him, as Monticello did to Jefferson. He managed to live there when Congress was not in session, and when away, sent long, minutely specific instructions to his overseers.

Was retirement feasible? The Union was prospering, despite perpetual troubles with the Indians along the frontier. But Federalist-Republican controversy was spreading, not diminishing. In a confidential talk, Madison urged Washington not to abandon the Presidency; no other figure – not even Madison's close friend Jefferson – could preserve unity. John Adams, the Vice-President, was suspect as a Federalist, a snob and a New Englander. John Jay, though he had fewer enemies, was also too much of a Federalist. Hamilton was out of the question, as the Arch-Federalist. Though Madison did not mention himself, he likewise, as a prominent Republican, was out of the running. Only Washington would do.

It was a disagreeable reflection. We cannot tell at what point Washington finally resigned himself to his fate. Possibly he clung to the notion that some candidate could be found, if only he could heal the breach between Hamilton and Jefferson. At any rate he took pains to clarify the situation. Jefferson supplied him with a list of no fewer than twenty-one charges against Hamilton, "the corrupt squadron of paper dealers" and Federalist tendencies in general ("The ultimate object of all this is to prepare the way for a change, from the present republican form of Government, to that of a monarchy; of which the British Constitution is to be the model"). Washington copied the items out and passed them on to Hamilton, without mention of Jefferson, implying that they were a summary of criticisms that had reached him from various sources. In due course Hamilton replied, angrily, eloquently and circumstantially, denying every one of the charges.

Washington persevered, urging both men in tactful language to sink their differences for the common good. Their answers were disappointingly truculent. Jefferson reiterated his previous charges and added fresh ones. Hamilton laid all the blame on Jefferson and would not undertake to drop his campaign against the Republicans. There was nothing much that Washington could do further, except renew his appeal for a spirit of mutual tolerance and persuade Jefferson not to retire from the Secretaryship of State. He did not wish to lose the services of either, for they were men of rare ability whose advice was almost indispensable to him. He may also have realized that out of office they would be equally active and more reckless.

And perhaps it occurred to Washington that, in office, they balanced one another to some extent. A "cabinet" without Jefferson would encourage Hamilton to spread himself. It would give color to the argument that a monarchy was in the making. Washington did not take this argument seriously. He had been a little shocked, and possibly bewildered, when a group of officers had hinted to him in 1783 that with their aid he could become King of the United States; there is little to suggest, though, that he believed such a scheme conceivable, in terms of himself or of any other American. Unlike Jefferson, he appears to have seen no harm in the fact that under the Constitution a President could in theory be re-elected several times. Yet if there were suspicions of monarchy, he was ready to allay them. As for a "cabinet" without Hamilton, this might encourage the Republicans to undo what Washington regarded as a Hamiltonian system of proven merit. Moreover, if a sectional and occupational bias could be attributed to Hamilton, the same could be said of Jefferson, who had declared his determination to uphold the South.

In short, Washington must retain his executive chiefs, and he must remain President (it was quite obvious that the electors would choose him in 1792, unless he begged them not to). If he needed the two factions to cancel one another out, he might have derived an ironical satisfaction from the thought that they needed him. Both Jefferson and Hamilton (as well as Randolph, Madison and others close to him) implored Washington to do his duty by the nation. Once more he was committed, and John Adams with him, to four years of lonely grandeur – one might almost say of penal servitude, so bleak was the prospect. He would uphold the Constitution at the expense of his own constitution. Must the road lead always away from Mount Vernon?

SECOND ADMINISTRATION: 1793-1797

Whether or not Washington guessed it, his second administration was to expose him to more criticism than he had suffered in his entire life. He had already, as President, been perturbed by faction in the country as a whole and faction within the government in particular. Now, as grave issues of foreign policy divided the nation, the discord was to become strident.

Not long after Washington's first inauguration in 1789, revolution broke out in France. In the autumn of 1792, while Washington was endeavoring to reconcile Hamilton and Jefferson, France proclaimed herself a republic. She had, in the eyes of sympathetic Americans, followed the example set by the United States – though with certain regrettable excesses; France's Declaration of the Rights of Man was lineally descended from Jefferson's Declaration of Independence; America was no longer the only democratic republic in the world. But a few weeks before Washington's second inauguration in March 1793, the French sent their former king, Louis XVI, to the guillotine and added Britain to the list of countries with which they were at war.

Here indeed was a crisis for infant America. She has never found neutrality easy to maintain; in fact, it has throughout her history proved almost impossible in the case of major European conflicts. In 1793 the situation was extraordinarily tense and delicate. On the one hand, France was America's late ally. Gratitude for Yorktown prompted the thought that the New World should rally to the republican cause in the Old. So did more precise obligations, since the United States was still bound to France by a treaty of alliance. Confronted by the spectacle of tyrannical Britain, her late enemy, at grips with egalitarian France, how could she fail to show her preference?

On the other hand, America had even more intimate ties with Britain. Until the War of Independence, the colonies, like the mother country, regarded France as the hereditary enemy. The winning of independence did not mean the severing of all connections with Britain. To many Americans (Hamilton prominent among them) the land of George III and William Pitt was still, with all her faults, a near relation. The bulk of American overseas trade was with the British Empire; if it were suspended, Hamilton's revenue system would collapse. Again, republicanism in America was a different proposition from republicanism in Europe, where it was ushered in by bloody revolution. American Tories were merely tarred and feathered; French *aristos,* like their king, perished on the scaffold. For a while Washington's dear friend Lafayette was among the leaders in France, until he fell into disgrace in 1792 and lay for four years in the dubious sanctuary of an Austrian jail. At that, he was luckier than most of his comrades.

America's obvious course, as Washington saw it and as even his quarreling advisers agreed at the outset, was to remain neutral; and this was the policy he promptly announced in a proclamation. As a polite concession to French opinion (and to Jefferson, who urged the point) he did not actually use the word "neutrality" in the document. He signified approval of the new French government by preparing to receive its minister, Citizen Genêt. So much was clear and precise; then for a while everything in America appeared to be an angry chaos. For if America was officially neutral, individual Americans were not. They had tended to take sides from the very outbreak of the French Revolution; now their enthusiasms were inflamed to an astonishing degree. "Gallomen" made Tom Paine's *Rights of Man* their Bible, damned aristocracy and harrahed for liberty, formed themselves into Democratic clubs and gave Genêt a tremendous welcome when he arrived on the scene. "Anglomen" watched in horror, and denounced their opponents as subversive madmen.

Even at a distance of a century and a half it is hard for us to see these events in perspective, or properly estimate Washington's part in them. To all but the extreme Federalists, he was both a hero and an emblem: the prestige of his name was their ultimate appeal in all argument. To all but moderate Republicans he became something of a tarnished warrior, the embodiment – willingly or unwillingly – of Federalist schemes and machinations. In 1793, for the first time in his long career, Washington was the target of sustained and open criticism. "God save great Washington," Americans had sung in 1789 (to the tune of "God save our Gracious King"). In 1793 they were reminding one another in Republican newspapers that he was no demigod, but a fallible mortal who had surrounded himself with "court satellites" and "mushroom lordlings." Two years later a Philadelphia journalist called Washington "a man in his political dotage" and "a supercilious tyrant." "If ever a nation was debauched by a man," the same journalist remarked at the end of 1796, "the American Nation has been debauched by Washington."

The bulk of contemporary comment was more respectful in tone. Yet these examples are a gauge of the passions of the era. The Republicans felt that the Chief Magistrate was being transformed into a party chieftain, and that under the guise of disinterested patriotism the Federalists were playing into the hands of the British. They admitted that France's conduct was puzzling, and even reprehensible; Genêt, for example, behaved so wildly that Jefferson was forced to concur with Washington in demanding his withdrawal. But they nevertheless preferred France to Britain, as they preferred the future to the past. They saw America cold to her true friend and deferential to her real enemy. With rage they heard in 1794 that Washington was sending John Jay, a known Federalist and Anglophile to London to negotiate a settlement of outstanding differences. Their worst suspicions were confirmed in March 1795, when details of the treaty he had signed reached America.

Instead of asserting America's rights, he seemed to have given way meekly. True, the British pledged themselves to evacuate the various western posts on American soil that they still held, and from which they were stirring up the Indians. But this was the only notable concession; and after all, the British were only undertaking to carry out a promise made more than ten years before. Otherwise, the concessions seemed to be on the American side. And several vital matters were deferred for future negotiations. The Anglomen were selling America's birthright; Jay was a traitor (they burned him in effigy); Federalists were villains; Washington was a "political hypocrite," not the Father but the "Step-Father" of His Country. Wrangling over Jay's Treaty went on through

1795 and part of 1796, long after the Senate ratified and Washington signed the document. In vain – the treaty came into effect and Jay was upheld. By contrast, the American envoy to France, James Monroe, a Virginian and a Republican, was recalled in disgrace by Washington in 1796, apparently for failure in the impossible task of convincing the French that Jay's Treaty was an American rather than a Federalist measure.

Such was the Republican view of foreign policy in Washington's second administration. At home they detected other evidence of Federalist malice. Hamilton's "odious" excise law (as Jefferson called it) provoked so much indignation that in 1792 Washington tried to reinforce it in a severely worded proclamation. Two years later, persuaded by Hamilton that the "whiskey rebels" of western Pennsylvania were threatening the safety of the Union, he called out a large militia force and sent it to the scene of the trouble, after inspecting the troops at their rendezvous. There was no fighting because – according to the Republicans – there was no real rebellion, only a phantom conjured up by Hamilton for his own purposes. A hundred and fifty Pennsylvanians were arrested; two were condemned to death. Washington pardoned them, yet he seemed to be converted to Hamilton's view. The game, in Madison's opinion, was "to connect the Democratic Societies with the odium of the insurrection – to connect the Republicans in Congress with those societies – to put the President ostensibly at the head of the other party." Jefferson, a year earlier, had actually told the President that Hamilton's intention was "to dismount him from being the head of the nation and to make him the head of a party." When Washington went so far as to lay the blame for the rebellion on "certain self-created societies," in his annual address to Congress of November 1794, Madison thought he had made "perhaps the greatest error of his political life."

So much for the Republican interpretation of events. What of Washington's standpoint? He was neither Angloman nor Galloman. This was a continuation of the war for independence, but must be fought without resort to war. The main threat to America's stability was external, for to a humiliating degree she still lacked an effective will of her own. America was not yet fully independent or mature. Like the adolescent heroine of some melodrama, she was heiress to a fortune of which false guardians struggled to deprive her, either by forcing her into matrimony or – if necessary – by murder.

Of the two self-appointed guardians France was the more dangerous. Britain was surly and contemptuous, flouting neutral rights in her typical style. But America could not afford to challenge Britain; the aim was to preserve trading relations and improve them, to get the redcoats out of the western forts, to avoid close commitments and in general to play for time. Though Washington was disappointed in Jay's performance, he recognized that America held too weak a hand to achieve miracles.

As for France, the menace was more subtle, and harder to combat. Washington's emphasis was on *neutrality*; the French stress was on *friendly* neutrality. They did not choose to invoke the existing treaty of alliance, because they expected to profit from the ambiguities of their link with the United States. They would get supplies. More important, they could employ America as a base for privateers and perhaps for imperial adventures in the Caribbean and the American hinterland. Genêt had both possibilities actively in mind, and like his successors, he assumed that he could depend on revolutionary sentiment in America to bolster him. If Washington and the Federalists stood in the way, France would appeal beyond them to the American people. In fact, by 1796 French agents in America were doing their best to ensure a Republican victory at the polls.

Washington's problems were complicated by partisan intrigue. Hamilton with deliberate indiscretion confided in British diplomatic representatives while the Republicans (though Jefferson himself was less at fault) tended to treat the French as full allies. Though Jefferson resigned from office at the end of 1793 and Hamilton at the beginning of 1795, their influence on national affairs continued to be felt. Hamilton in particular maintained his hold – partly, it must be admitted, at Washington's invitation. He contrived, while running a law practice in New York, to remain as a sort of invisible cabinet member. Jefferson's successor as Secretary of State, Edmund Randolph, had to be dismissed in 1795 in peculiar circumstances. Rightly or wrongly, Washington thought him guilty of conspiring with the French minister against Jay's treaty.

However, despite intrigues, blandishments and frank abuse, Washington stuck to his policy. We must conclude that in the light of subsequent history – a light, of course, denied him – he was right, and that the extreme Republicans, at any rate, who would have pulled America into the French orbit, were wrong, even if for worthy motives. He was wise, he was courageous; if he now and then lost his temper, he did not lose his grip. Nor was his diplomacy entirely negative in its results. The meager gains of Jay were handsomely offset in Thomas Pinckney's treaty with Spain in 1795, by which at long last America won acceptance of the claim to free navigation of the Mississippi (whose outlet was in Spanish territory) and of the recognition of the Mississippi as her western boundary. An Indian treaty of the same year, following a decisive victory won by General Anthony Wayne in what is now Ohio, brought additional security to the northwestern frontier. "With me," Washington was to reiterate in his Farewell Address, "a predominant motive has been, to endeavor to gain time to our country to settle and mature its yet recent institutions, and to progress without interruption to that degree of strength and consistency, which is necessary to give it, humanly speaking, the command of its own fortunes."

Given these conditions, the country could not fail to forge ahead. Washington saw proofs of growth and prosperity all around him. By the end of his second administration three new states – Vermont, Kentucky and Tennessee – had joined the Union, and others would follow. Turnpike roads were under construction; coal deposits had been found in Pennsylvania; though progress was slow, the Potomac Company was still alive, as were other improvement schemes; and the Federal City (in which Washington took a keen interest) was being laid out, in a mingled atmosphere of grandeur and pettiness that may have set the tone of the place for ever afterward.

For these accomplishments Washington is entitled to take much of the credit – although he did not claim it – since a less consistent foreign policy would have jeopardized them all. With the passage of Jay's Treaty the French became increasingly hostile, until the tension at home and abroad was almost unendurable. The Vice-President's son, John Quincy Adams, writing from Holland (where he was American minister), said at the end of 1795 that "if our neutrality be still preserved, it will be due to the President alone. Nothing but his weight of character and reputation, combined with his firmness and political intrepidity, could have stood against the torrent that is still tumbling with a fury that resounds even across the Atlantic."

If we grant that Washington revealed fine powers of leadership in these years of crisis, is it true that he did so as leader of a political party – the Federalists – rather than as a dispassionate Chief Magistrate? We have noted that, in common with most of his contemporaries, he considered parties as undesirable phenomena; that he saw the President as above politics; and that above all he wished to establish law and order in the Union. The vigor of republican opposition was an unpleasant surprise, though he felt able to hold the balance so long as Republican attacks were concentrated upon Hamilton. But during his second administration, as political controversy grew and as he himself came under fire, Washington's opinions gradually hardened. "I think," said Jefferson, "he feels those things more than any other person I ever met with." Washington burst out, at a cabinet meeting in 1793, that Freneau was a "rascal" who ought to be stopped. Freneau's newspaper did cease publication later in the year, but other Republican sheets kept up the offensive. Resenting criticism, as always, and believing with some reason that the Republicans were irresponsible and malevolent, Washington came at length to share the Federalist view that their opponents were not the *other* party, but simply "party," or "faction"; not the "opposition" who might one day justly inherit the reins of government, but opposition as sedition, conspiracy, Gallomania. Hence his too sweeping condemnation of the Democratic societies, most of which were harmless political clubs; hence his indignant comment in a letter of 1798 that "you could as soon scrub the blackamore white, as to change the principles of a profest Democrat," and that such a man "will leave nothing unattempted to overturn the Government of this Country." His final cabinet was entirely Federalist in composition.

From this it was only a step – a step that, nevertheless, he probably took unconsciously – to acknowledging that he himself was a Federalist. In 1799, the last year of his life, when he had been out of office for two years, Washington was urged to stand as a candidate in the presidential election of 1800, on the grounds that the Union was in grave danger. He refused, explaining that "principle, not men, is now, and will be, the object of contention." Even if he put himself forward, "I should not draw a *single* vote from the Anti-federal side; and of course, should stand upon no stronger ground than any other Federal well supported." He was not quite ready to concede that the Republicans were a legitimate group; yet from his letter as a whole ("any *other* Federal") we see that he was beginning to grasp the altered basis of American politics.

If he had still been in office, he might not have been willing to label himself a Federalist; he might have maintained that the President must still stand aloof. Certainly no serious blame attaches to him; but on this issue he did not achieve the lofty and prescient calm that some biographers have acclaimed in him. Only by seeing the decade entirely through Washington's or through Federalist eyes can we agree that he justly formulated the political equation.

THE LAST RETIREMENT

These are speculative matters. Whatever else is doubtful, though, there can be no doubt that Washington was profoundly glad to relinquish the Presidency. Many expected him to accept a third term, and everyone knew that he could be re-elected with ease. Despite some hostile comment, he was still by far the most admired of Americans. But he had had enough – more than enough. His successor, John Adams, while flattered by the honor, was under no illusion as to what lay ahead. "A solemn scene it was indeed," Adams wrote to his wife, describing the inauguration in March 1797, "and it was made affecting to me by the presence of the General, whose countenance was as serene and unclouded as the day. He seemed to enjoy a triumph over me. Methought I heard him say, 'Ay! I am fairly out and you fairly in! See which of us will be the happiest!' . . . In the chamber of the House of Representatives was a multitude as great as the space would contain, and I believe scarcely a dry eye but Washington's." Washington had been deeply moved on other great occasions – as when he said good-by to his officers at Fraunces' Tavern in 1783. No tears now; all that he noted in his diary, under the inaugural date, was "Much such a day as yesterday in all respects. Mercury at 41."

It was not that he handed over office in a sulk, but that nothing and no one could now convince him that he was indispensable to America. He had just celebrated his sixty-fifth birthday (or rather, it had just been celebrated for him, at an "elegant entertainment" where twelve hundred Philadelphians squeezed in to applaud him) and did not expect to enjoy many more. The few years that were left he meant to spend at Mount Vernon. His adult life had been splendid; yet the passage of time and the demand of public service had consumed too much. Most of his old friends were dead. One of the Fairfaxes had come back to Virginia, but Belvoir was a ruin and Sally Fairfax had never returned from England. Lafayette was free again (Washington had sent funds to his wife, with habitual generosity), but an ocean away. There remained Mount Vernon and the cheerful companionship of Martha and some of their young relatives.

If biography could be made as shapely as a good play, we could ring the curtain gently down on Washington, leaving him in white-haired tranquility. His existence, however, was not cast in such a pattern. The curtain was always jerking up again, the music awakening suddenly from some lulling coda. So it was to be again with him in 1798. In a way, it was his own fault. He would have been left alone if he had seemed senile. Instead, he appeared as vigorous as ever, whether in superintending his farms, in offering hospitality, or in dealing with correspondence. His letters, in fact, seem more pungent – perhaps because he now felt more at liberty to speak his mind, whereas hitherto official caution had hedged him in. At any rate, he was summoned back into uniform in 1798. French conduct had grown so outrageous that she was virtually at war with the United States. At naval war, that is. America had no army, except for the tiny nucleus of regulars that Washington had struggled to retain. He was now required to raise an army and assume command. The prospect made him groan. When Hamilton predicted that another summons to action would reach him, Washington replied that he would go "with as much reluctance from my presence peaceful abode, as I should do to the tomb of my ancestors." He was displeased when President Adams nominated him as commander in chief without previous consultation. He was worried, as before in his career, that opponents might interpret his return to authority as a piece of ambition or – in view of his Farewell Address – hypocrisy. But the obligation was not to be evaded. Brisk, sensible, conscientious, he set about the task. As before, the ubiquitous Alexander Hamilton was promptly on hand, arranging things behind the scenes, securing for himself an appointment that would make him Washington's second-in-command. It was a hectic time, especially for poor John Adams. In his place, Washington would probably have come in for similar vilification. But we can be fairly sure that Washington would have avoided some of Adams's tactical blunders in the business of administration. A detailed comparison of his Presidency with Washington's would do much to bring out the solid, sober merit of the latter.

However, there was no war in 1798 or in 1799. Washington's life resumed its normal tempo. The months wheel by in the jog-trot entries of his diary. Hot days, cool days, rain, snow. Surveying, riding, visitors, dinners, a baby daughter born to Martha's granddaughter Eleanor Custis Lewis. Then the diary stops on December 13, with a note that the thermometer has dropped to a slight frost. Then, indeed, the curtain comes down with a rush. Washington has caught a chill; he has a sore throat; the doctors bleed him, bleed him again, to no avail. At ten in the evening of December 14 he is dead, without a climax (save for that invented posthumously by Parson Weems), without a memorable final utterance; in pain, a sacrifice to the well-meaning but barbarous medical treatment of his day.

With less primitive care he could have survived a few more years. He could have witnessed the removal of the federal government to the Federal City (christened Washington, D.C.), which would have pleased him, or the inauguration of Thomas Jefferson in 1801, following a Republican victory that would not have pleased him. He could have read of the Louisiana Purchase, and of Hamilton's death in a duel – a medley of bright news and dark news. But would he have wanted much more? His century was over, and he with it. Spenser's quiet lines fit his end better than many of the sonorous phrases that orators and scribes (including Freneau) were soon declaiming throughout the enormous, ramshackle, thriving Union:

Sleep after toyle, port after stormie seas,
Ease after warre, death after life does greatly please.

CHAPTER FIVE
THE WHOLE MAN

George Washington had thanks and naught beside.
Except the all-cloudless glory (which few men's is)
To free his country.

BYRON, *Don Juan,* Canto IX

Shall we make an Idol of him, and worship it with huzzahs on the Fourth of July, and with stupid Rhetoric on other days? Shall we build him a great monument, founding it in a slave pen?

THEODORE PARKER, *Historic Americans* (1870)

The head of Washington hangs in my dining-room for a few days past, and I cannot keep my eyes off it. It has a certain Appalachian strength, as if it were truly the first-fruits of America and expressed the Country. The heavy, leaden eyes turn on you, as the eyes of an ox in a pasture. And the mouth has gravity and depth of quiet, as if this MAN had absorbed all the serenity of America, and left none for his restless, rickety, hysterical countrymen.

RALPH WALDO EMERSON, *Journals,* July 6, 1849

RETICENCE

Having pored over the record and set down their impressions, most biographers of George Washington are still left with the uneasy sense that something has escaped them. It is not that the record is fragmentary or contradictory. We know what Washington was doing at every period of his life, once he emerged from childhood. We can make a reasonable rough guess at what he may have been thinking on almost any occasion. His activities as a prewar planter would become somewhat clearer if we had to hand letters sent by his English agent, Robert Cary of London. And perhaps we should have more intimate insights if the correspondence with his wife Martha had been preserved, or if (according to Dixon Wecter) J. P. Morgan's secretary-librarian had not on one occasion fed a batch of allegedly "smutty" letters to the furnace. But one doubts whether these would materially have altered the picture. Some episodes in Washington's career – notably during his Presidency – have not yet been exhaustively analyzed. Even so, the material for a full-length portrait is there, both in his own words and in abundant comment about him.

Why, then, the enigma, the confession that George Washington has eluded us? Why, when all the lineaments seem sharp, is the portrait so strangely opaque? There are two main reasons: the nature of his personality and the vast shadow thrown by the Washington legend – the Washington Monument. His personality baffles because it presents the mystery of no mystery. In examining the careers of the great, we are accustomed to look for – and to find – disguised clues or evidences of frailty. We can discern in some the passionate ambition of the parvenu, or the truculence common in men of small physique. Both of these factors help to explain the behavior of an Alexander Hamilton or Napoleon. Others are possessed by an ideological demon; they have heard voices, whose peremptory summons they follow to the death, if need be. In some the will to action springs from deeply secret sources (as, for instance, in the hidden homosexuality of the British hero General Gordon). In most, the splendor is offset by a blemish – promiscuity, avarice, vanity. Yet what clues do we need or can we detect to uncover Washington – tall, handsome gentleman of middling views, modest, abstemious, culprit in nothing except perhaps an early and circumspect longing for Sally Fairfax? A reputation for tight-fistedness is the worst personal failing that he has been at all plausibly accused of. Through forged correspondence during the Revolutionary War, the British tried to spread the rumor that Washington was a concealed Tory, also that he had mistresses here and there, black and white. Another piece of British rumor-mongering claimed that Washington was in fact a woman disguised in man's clothes. This absurd item gained some slight credence as an explanation of his having fathered no offspring by Martha, though she had conceived four children in her first marriage. The assorted "Washington scandals," however, yield nothing to the investigator. They either lack any corroboration, or can be shown to have been deliberate fabrications.

Was he, then, a mediocrity? The monument inhibits an answer. Each would-be impartial historian must either, it appears, surrender to conventional piety or else descend to petty fault-finding. It is not much consolation to reflect that the same awkward choice, between adulation and vandalism, faced Washington's contemporaries.

Grappling with the problem, some biographers have solved it by denying that it exists; by stressing, that is, the "human" qualities of the man. Thus, to Bradley T. Johnson, "Washington was a man all over – a man with strong appetites, fierce temper, positive, belligerent, and aggressive"; Rupert Hughes maintains that Washington was actually "one of the most eager, versatile, human men that ever lived"; to Saul K. Padover he is a "passionate, sensitive, earthy, deeply feeling human being"; and to Howard Swiggett, in a book entitled *The Great Man George Washington as a Human Being* (1953), its hero is a compound of "magnetism and grandeur, cold fury and biting wit, goodness and charity, troubles and woe . . . believing in dignity and decorum but able to laugh at or discard them." This is the approach that dwells on his reckless courage; or upon his eloquent swearing at Monmouth Court House, that day of intolerable heat and vexation when he is supposed to have called Charles Lee, a "damned poltroon"; or upon his popularity with women, his fondness for dancing and so on.

The emphasis is not without value. It provides a useful corrective to the genuflections of earlier biographers like Marshall, Weems and

Sparks. We can do without the absurder items in the Washington legend – the cherry tree, the prayer at Valley Forge and the rest. It is especially important in going behind the Washington of the Stuart portrait to the younger and far less eminent man, the vulnerable adolescent, the energetic surveyor, the busy colonel of Virginia Militia, the planter in love with his new estates.

In this part of his life, as Douglas Southall Freeman has shown, we *can* separate the man from the monument and trace the development of his character. We can note how his family, though respectable, did not take rank with the grandees of the colony (we might say facetiously that Washington was born not with a silver but with a silver-plated spoon in his mouth, and was soon deprived of that by his father's death); how he had to shift for himself, with a measure of assistance from his relatives and from the powerful Fairfaxes; how his ambitions (and he *was* ambitious) were thus formed, then heightened by the prospect of a military career, then thwarted by his failure to secure the patronage of British regulars (Braddock's death at the Monongahela may have been a serious setback for Washington, whatever subsequent glory he gained from his own conduct in the defeat), then mellowed by a prosperous marriage; how he hence became both a gentleman of standing and a decently libertarian product of the Enlightenment, who when required to choose for or against the mother country was able to reach a decision by logical degrees and without undue anguish. We can see how he profited by the mistakes of immaturity, growing gradually in dignity and self-control.

In each of us there are numerous buried selves from our past. His Virginia experiences were buried within George Washington, and it does not seem fanciful to argue that there always remained alive in him a vestige of early fire. Another young Virginian who also became President, Woodrow Wilson, told his fiancée in 1884, "It isn't pleasant or convenient to have strong passions. I have the uncomfortable feeling that I am carrying a volcano about with me." Similar words might have been applied to young Washington, though, as with Wilson, the mature man presented an austere front to the world. According to James T. Flexner, among recent biographers, Washington may in fact have been sterile. This must remain merely a theory. There is nothing in his behavior, though, to suggest that he was impotent, or that his sexual nature caused him any deep uneasiness.

However, there is a latent error in stressing the "human" side of Washington. We are likely to substitute for a nineteenth-century copybook version of the man a twentieth-century version which is equally misleading as a description of a figure who was, after all, of the *eighteenth* century. Let us admit that Washington had the tastes of a squire of the more refined sort; that he liked food, wine and company, a game of cards, the theater, a race meeting, fox hunting; that he had a sense of humor, if a little on the heavy side; that he enjoyed the admiration of women, as expressed in the lightly affectionate correspondence of a Philadelphia friend, Mrs. Eliza Powel; and that he had emotions which now and then were touched to the point of tears. Concede this much, and it still does not follow that Washington was anything like our current Hollywood-and-historical-novel conception of an American hero.

He was brave, but he was not a wildcat. He knew the frontier, and the advantages of dressing like a frontiersman in the appropriate circumstances, but he was no Davy Crockett. In British eyes he was a rebel, yet never in his own. Nor did he think of himself as a revolutionary. When Lafayette sent him the key of the Bastille, to symbolize the overthrow of despotism, Washington responded merely with a polite acknowledgment and a token gift in return.

> Not for the value of the thing, my dear Marquis, but as a memorial, and because they are the manufacture of this city, I send you herewith a pair of shoe-buckles.

A pair of shoe-buckles – what inspired flatness!

Washington was in some respects a plain, unassuming man; visitors to Mount Vernon remarked with surprise on the simplicity of the dress he wore when out on the farms. But, they also remarked, he changed for dinner. He was not an intellectual, but he was not impatient of intellect in others. If sometimes inelegantly phrased, his conversation and his letters were by no means couched in the idiom of the coonskin democrat. If he swore, he did so only in rare moments of stress and without habitual gusto (there is, incidentally, no reliable foundation for the story that he let loose his tongue on Lee at Monmouth), to judge from the rare reports that have come down to us.

He could be genial, but he did not whoop it up. In all his life, so far as we can tell, he had no bosom friend of his own age. Washington opened his heart to Lafayette – there is a rare sprightliness in his correspondence with the Frenchman – and he had a particularly fond regard for his young Carolinian staff officer, John Laurens, who was killed in the Revolutionary War; yet his relations with both were paternal, or at any rate avuncular.

In contrast with ours, Washington's was a reticent era. Compare him, though, even with his contemporaries and the difference in manner is striking. If Washington is "passionate, sensitive, earthy," then Franklin, Jefferson, Madison and Hamilton – not to mention a Patrick Henry or an Aaron Burr – are rip-roarers and hellions. Listen to the verdict of foreign observers. A Dutchman who came to Mount Vernon in 1784 "had the desire to appreciate him" but concluded, "I could never be on familiar terms with the General – a man so cold, so cautious, so obsequious." Another European who met Washington four years later said of him, "There seemed to me to skulk somewhat of a repulsive coldness, not congenial with my mind, under a courteous demeanour." Jefferson likewise, in a far from hostile summary, remarked that Washington's heart was "not warm in its affections." In part this was shyness; with close acquaintances he could seem more at ease. But we can hardly accept the notion of Washington as a glad-hander at any period of his career. Perhaps it is unfair to cite as typical the fact that at the end of his life he approved of the drastic Alien and Sedition Acts – in this, going beyond Alexander Hamilton in the severity of his conservatism. Still, at a much earlier age, when he was about to retire from Virginia soldiering, it is apparent that to the officers of his regiment (some older than he) their young colonel was admired from a distance. They looked up to him, not sideways at him. Washington was no one's buddy; he was not "just folks."

In short, to humanize Washington is to run the risk of falsifying – of losing the essential truth of his personality. Interestingly enough, most of his nineteenth-century biographers – even Weems, to some extent – were conscious that their task was to make Washington credible as well as heroic; to convey his strengths without resorting to adulatory stuff. In 1856 the historian William H. Prestcott congratulated Washington Irving for skillful compromise: "You have done with Washington just as I thought you would, and, instead of a cold, marble statue of a demigod, you have made him a being of flesh and blood, like ourselves – one with whom we can have sympathy." Replying to another congratulatory letter, Irving said: "I have availed myself of the licence of biography to step down occasionally from the elevated walk of history, and relate familiar things in a familiar way, seeking to . . . depict the heroes of Seventy-Six as they really were – men in cocked hats, regimental coats, and breeches, and not classic warriors in shining armor and flowing mantles, with brows bound with laurel. . . ."

In lectures given by the Boston clergyman-abolitionist Theodore Parker, in 1858, he praised Washington for integrity and administrative

Virginian one). Gravitas, pietas, simplicitas, integritas and gloria were other valued Roman qualities.

As the virtue, so the environment. Rome was a martial civilization, always aware of the unrest along the frontiers, the bringer of law and imposer of order. Roman culture was a trifle hard and unsubtle, or at any rate rooted in reality rather than raptly poetic; religious feeling was moderate in tone, excess being deplored. Rome was a slave-holding society in which (outside the capital and the provincial centers) the unit of neighborhood was a farm estate. It was a society that relied upon the family as the cohesive force. Affection, respect, loyalty, spread outward from the family, which was thus the state in microcosm. This was a society that bred solid, right-thinking citizens, at once civic and acquisitive, men of a noble narrowness, seeing further than their noses but not agitating themselves with vain speculation. Such are the implications of words like *gravitas* (seriousness), *pietas* (regard for discipline and authority), *simplicitas* (lucidity).

For "Rome" here, may we not read "Virginia"? And were Washington's old-style biographers, or the admirers of his own generation, so wildly wrong when they said he was set in the antique mold, Cincinnatis reborn?[9] The broad picture of him as soldier, landowner, statesman all in one is Roman; Cincinnatus is among many Roman heroes who combined these functions. So are the details Roman. There is something of Rome in Washington's attachment to Mount Vernon, his dutiful, if unenthusiastic concern for his mother, his uncomplaining and constant attention to the welfare of the multifarious brood of Washington brothers and sisters, cousins, nephews, nieces, stepchildren and other kinsmen. Generosity, yes (the very origin of the word is Latin, and takes us back to the *gens*, or clan); yet more than mere good nature – a positive call to duty.

Duty. Here is another Roman clue to Washington: duty seen as a cluster of obligations. Obligations, be it noted, rather than some more modern word such as "compulsions"; for these are not individual but

---

[9] It was not merely empty rhetoric that led old Daniel Webster, invoking the memory of Washington in face of threatened disunion (July 4, 1851), to close with a fragmentary quotation from Roman oratory: Duo modo haec opto: unum, ui moriens populum liberum relinquam; hoc mihi maius a diis immortalibus dari nihil potest; alterum, ut ita cuique eveniat, ut de republica quisque mereatur (I wish these things: one, that in dying I may leave a free people; nothing greater than this can be given me by the immortal gods; the second, that each man may prove worthy of the republic). Fisher Ames's funeral oration to Washington (Boston, 1800) reached back through Plutarch to the Greek city states: "Some future Plutarch will search for a parallel to his character. Epaminondas is perhaps the brightest name of all antiquity. Our Washington resembled him in the purity and ardor of his patriotism; and like him, he first exalted the glory of his country. There it is to be hoped the parallel ends; for Thebes fell with Epaminondas."

social necessities, and Washington was, if not a particularly sociable man, nevertheless emphatically a social being, a member though not a joiner. The personality that emerges from the pattern – once mature – is stoical to the point of frigidity, and yet complete, poised, even serene: this is the implication of *integritas*. It may own some doubts, but no crippling ones; the rules of decent behavior will supply an answer to the toughest problems. Courage becomes automatic, death a fate without terrors.

> It is the duty then of a thinking man to be neither superficial, nor impatient, nor yet contemptuous in his attitude towards death, but to await it as one of the operations of Nature which he will have to undergo.

Marcus Aurelius said this; Washington could have, as he made his will, issued his Farewell Address to the American people, and repaired the Mount Vernon vault in readiness for the inevitable.

As for ambition – *gloria* – it is conceived as a civic impulse, not a private torment. Certainly this is true of Washington once he had got over his young man's hunger for notice and preferment. Again, Washington's desire to be well thought of and to keep his reputation unsullied is a classical desire, not tin the least akin to the populist, "other-directed" anxiousness that renders prominent men of the present day so susceptible to the idea of public opinion – an oracle thought to be enshrined in polls, best-seller lists and the like. True, Washington while a soldier consulted his officers before fastening upon a plan; and as President he tried to keep in touch with the mood of the country. At critical moments, however, especially during the tumult over Jay's treaty, he acted in the manner of a high-minded Roman, unhesitating. He spoke of "the People" without disdain, but with no Rousseauistic *frisson*.

It would be idle to pretend that Washington's Virginia simply repeated the modes and experiences of the ancient world, or that all his contemporaries were as markedly "classical" in temperament. The point is that his age differed profoundly from ours; that in certain ways he is better understood within a classical framework than as a man of modern times; and that his planter Virginia was in a way more truly "Roman" than the mother country. The Rome sketched here is an ideal image of a society whose values were severely practical; and this is the impression we finally retain of Washington's character – a type of character that is unfamiliar to our generation. In historical terms the parallel is approximate; in poetic terms it is close, and helps us to grasp why men such as Washington believed that they could create a huge new nation on the republican model. Though initially they were loyal subjects of George III, their environment and habits of thought led them by natural if imperceptible degrees away from kings and courtiers, away from Europe to a new order that was in effect a restatement of their existing situation. The lessons of the classical past, when the world was young, as America felt itself to be young, suggested that such a republic was a working possibility, as well as providing a warning that things might go wrong. Theirs was revolution, therefore, by conservation; Americans wished to reaffirm old values – simplicity, modesty and the like – in a fresh setting. The aim was both novel and traditional.

While Rome was an object lesson, it was not a blueprint for the infant nation. Many things were needed to make the successful transition from monarchy to republicanism and from the loose congeries of ex-colonies to the strong Union that emerged in the 1790s. Independence had to be fought for and then made real. It could be said that America became a nation legally before it was one emotionally. The word *Americanization*, now usually taken to refer to American influence over the rest of the world, was first coined in Washington's day to describe the defensive struggle of Americans to be something other than *Europeanized*. And in this respect, of course, the colonies owed much also to a sober, strong-willed character type engendered by the Protestant heritage. Nathaniel Hawthorne's description of New England leaders in the seventeenth century (in *The Scarlet Letter*) has some application to the Anglo-America represented in the eighteenth century by Washington's Virginia. "These primitive statesmen," as Hawthorne calls them, were "distinguished by a ponderous sobriety. . . . They had fortitude and self-reliance, and, in time of difficulty or peril, stood up for the welfare of the state like a line of cliffs against a tempestuous tide." They were physically strong and large. "So far as a demeanor of natural authority was concerned, the mother country need not have been ashamed to see these foremost men of an actual democracy adopted into the House of Peers, or made the Privy Council of the sovereign."

No wonder, then, that Washington was revered as much for what he was as for what he did. No wonder that he was turned into a monumental legend during his own lifetime. Within a few months of assuming command in 1775, General Washington occupied a unique position, a position extended and consolidated as the war years dragged on. It was not merely that he was a good soldier or a competent administrator. No direct inspiration passed from him to his soldiers; his courage was edifying, yet lacked the contagious, electric quality of leadership possessed by some military figures. His orders of the day did not make men cry *Ha, ha* to the sound of the trumpets, though they often provided food for thought; the general orders of July 9, 1776, after announcing a parade at which the Declaration of Independence was to be read, "with an audible voice" to the "several brigades," closed with the reminder to every officer and enlisted man that "he is now in the service of a State, possessed of sufficient power to reward his merit, and advance him to the highest Honors of a free Country." Was Washington remembering his own frustrations in the service of Virginia? Perhaps.

Were his words a little dull? Perhaps. That may be their significance, the solid underpinning to the eloquence of Jefferson's preamble. No one could feel that Washington was cheap; his gentlemanly restraint, his proven integrity, his whole record, proclaimed otherwise. He looked and behaved like a classical hero; on him hung the issue of America's posterity; and yet this figure who thus linked past and future linked them by occupying himself doggedly with the present, by being magnificently matter-of-fact. He symbolized America, but never was a symbol more real, more tangible, more explicit. Jefferson spoke of life, liberty and the pursuit of happiness, Washington of pay and promotion as a factor in patriotism. His very literalness brought actuality to the project of independence, dispelling the air of forlorn daydream that sometimes hung over the scene. He took for granted what even visionaries were unsure of: that a nation would emerge, and that it would prosper. And, paradoxically, the man who had his feet so firmly on the ground was gradually wafted into the clouds by his fellow countrymen. According to the *Pennsylvania Journal*, in 1777:

> If there are spots in his character, they are like the spots in the sun, only discernible by the magnifying powers of a telescope. Had he lived in the days of idolatry, he had been worshipped as a god.

CRITICISMS

Some Americans thought that he *was* being worshiped.

> I have been distressed to see some members of this house disposed to idolize an image which their own hands have molten. I speak here of the superstitious veneration that is sometimes paid to General Washington. Altho' I honour him for his good qualities, yet in this house I feel myself his Superior.

The writer was John Adams, also in 1777, when he was a member of the Continental Congress.

This situation deserves to be examined more closely, for we can learn much about Washington from it. In the first place, who were his most vocal critics? During the war, as we might expect, hostility came mainly from military subordinates and from their friends in Congress. Then and after, a high proportion were men who could be described as intellectuals, or at any rate as quick-witted men. It would be too strong to say that they detested or despised him; some had only mild reservations. Yet such men as Joseph Reed, Edmund Randolph, Alexander Hamilton, Aaron Burr (all onetime secretaries or aides), Timothy Pickering (his adjutant general), Benjamin Rush and others commented at different stages on his short-comings. What they intended to think is shrewdly summarized by the biographer James Parton, writing of Aaron Burr:

> He thought Washington . . . a very honest and well-intentioned country gentleman; but no great soldier, and very far indeed from being a demi-god. Burr disliked a dull person next to a coward, and he thought General Washington a dull person. Hamilton and other young soldier-scholars of the Revolution were evidently of a similar opinion, but Hamilton thought that the popularity of the general was essential to the triumph of the cause, and accordingly, he kept his opinion to himself.[10]

As a class, they were irked to realize that a man of so little intellectual distinction should have gained such renown. When he returned to public duty in 1787, some complained (perforce in private letters) that it had become impossible to oppose him without incurring the accusation of disloyalty to America. Others, including Hamilton, relied on this fact to win their arguments, sheltering behind the monument. John Adams contended (in 1785):

> Instead of adoring a Washington, mankind should applaud the nation which educated him. . . . I glory in the character of a Washington, because I know him to be only an exemplification of the American character. . . . In the days of Pompey, Washington would have been a Caesar; his officers and partisans

[10] Much the same polite cynicism as to Washington is conveyed in Gore Vidal's sparkling historical novel Burr – though, to be sure, Vidal's Aaron Burr is not much impressed by other contemporaries, including Thomas Jefferson.

would have stimulated him to it . . . in the time of Charles, a Cromwell; in the days of Philip the second, a prince of Orange, and would have wished to be Count of Holland. But in America he could have had no other ambition but that of retiring.

Reverence for Washington, then, was unjustified, silly – and dangerous. Unless Americans kept a sense of proportion, they would vote themselves back into monarchy and its attendant ills. Most of Washington's critics admitted that the peril lay in the precedent; adulation could become habitual. Washington himself was not, they conceded, swollen with conceit and never would be. Nevertheless, as his reputation grew, he was acquiring a kind of civic glaze. He was receding from humankind; far too much protocol surrounded him as President.

We may discount most of these assertions as the product of jealousy and party spirit. Old Franklin's grandson Benjamin Franklin Bache, editor of the Philadelphia *Aurora,* was implacably and exaggeratedly hostile. Yet his verbal assault on President Washington, however vindictive, had a rational base. Bache genuinely believed that the nation was in peril; and that the President was allowing it to slip back into monarchical, pro-British styles. Adams was right, in his ungracious way, when he said that Washington's abnegation was not so much a supreme act of disinterest as a proof that Americans were determined to enjoy a free republican form of government (not that Washington claimed any such credit). Adams was right, too, though again churlish, when he questioned Washington's refusal to accept any pay – other than expenses – while commander in chief. It seems evident that Washington did thereby lift himself somewhat above the role of public servant. Washington was actuated by the highest motives. He was scrupulous in deferring to the Continental Congress as his ultimate master. Even so, he differentiated himself from the other generals appointed under his command. They were appointed, as he had been, by Congress; and like them, he could be removed by Congress (except during the special periods of emergency when Congress granted him exceptional powers). However, what was for him altruism could possibly have been interpreted otherwise; and at least some of the exasperation and so-called plotting of Gates, Conway and other generals arose from their conviction that Washington regarded himself as irremovable.

In his own eyes, and those of most Americans, it was a matter of pure patriotism. He had merged his honor with that of America. Suppose, though, that he should make some disastrous blunder: could he really be dismissed? This was the sort of problem that engaged Adams and other members of the Continental Congress. Not that they had any serious intention of dismissing him; but they must have noticed that at no time in the war did he make even a gesture toward resigning. Why, they might wonder, did it not occur to him at the time of the Conway Cabal, in order to secure a vote of confidence, or, say, after Yorktown, when active warfare had ceased?

The answer is that, given his high sense of duty, he could not. He was justified in believing that American resistance might collapse once his control was gone. Yet the longer he remained at the helm, the more irrevocably did he become involved in and symbolic of the commonwealth. Crudely speaking, General Washington disappeared as a person to make way for a phenomenon, that of American Saint George. He was the victim of the process, but to some extent he brought it on himself, not merely by being so victorious, so calmly statesmanlike in manner, so disinterestedly national in outlook, but also by deliberately and avowedly surrendering his private identity. Being the man he was, he could not have done anything else. But the consequences, however much he groaned and protested, were equally unavoidable. Having once come to epitomize America, he was trapped in public life as a self-perpetuating candidate. Nothing but death, illness or disgrace could save the commander in chief from re-emerging as the President.

This, to reiterate, was not an outcome he planned, or perhaps even foresaw. His dissatisfactions under the Articles of Confederation did not, as with other famous men in retirement, derive from a craving to be back in charge of events. In 1788-89 his associates had to plead with him to accept the burdens of office. In 1792 they made similar efforts, including an intimation that perhaps he need not serve out a full term, to persuade him to remain at the helm. He offered to serve without pay, and indeed treated his presidential annual salary of $25,000 as a kind of expense allowance. Certainly he showed increasing distaste for the post of Chief Executive. James T. Flexner suggests that Washington was preoccupied with the onset of old age. Perhaps because of the early deaths of his father and his half-brother Lawrence, George believed his family was not long-lived. He took seriously the reaching of the "Grand Climacteric" – the age of sixty-three – in 1795. If teeth were a gauge of health, George's were no cause for optimism. The clumsy dentures designed for him in 1789 were built around his one remaining natural tooth. This did not long survive; and the dentures themselves collapsed at the beginning of 1797. It was as if these inner defenses were giving way, at the same time that opposition journalists were attacking the external image.

As President, Washington the man was thus still more irrevocably lost in Washington the monument. Here again the comments of his critics are not entirely unjustified. As Bache and other writers claimed during the President's increasingly unhappy second term, he was treating his salary as an account on which he could draw – or occasionally overdraw – in advance, a privilege not allowed to any other person. It was embarrassing enough to have a demigod in their midst; it was infuriating when the demigod became the property of the Federalists. This person was elevated so far above the political hurly-burly that he appeared to assume as of right that no electoral vote could possibly be cast against him, in 1789 or in 1792. In the Republican view of affairs, a man who was unassailable was now the patron saint of a policy that was intolerable. While Washington, in office, never publicly admitted that he too was a Federalist, he did lend his formidable prestige to the Federalist cause, simply by assuming that there was no other acceptable cause. After his death, Republicans were to witness the effort by Federalists to exploit the heroic legend by means of the Washington Benevolent Societies, which were political clubs disguised as hagiology (the societies' handbooks invariably included the text of Washington's Farewell Address). Americans were markedly reluctant to attack him – the speeches of Republicans in Congress are full of nervous disclaimers and preliminary compliments – but such attacks as they did deliver are not altogether attributable to spleen. They wished to sing his praises but were worried by the possible results. Behind his Federalist entourage, Washington did seem to harden, to grow less approachable and more disposed to resent outspoken opposition. Was there not a painful irony in the Pennsylvania Whiskey Rebellion of 1794, when half the men arrested under the President's edict came from a county named, in his honor, *Washington?*

David Meade, a brother of Washington's aide Richard Meade, had once said of the commander in chief that, "of a saturnine temperament, he was . . . better endowed by nature and habit for an Eastern monarch, than a republican general." In times of Republican-Federalist controversy such a remark had still more application. Alexander Hamilton's Act for Establishing a Mint proposed in 1792 that Washington's head should be stamped upon all coins of the United States. There is no evidence, or likelihood, that Washington himself strongly favored the idea. But to the Republicans, who managed to defeat the proposal, it was typical of an ominous trend in hero worship.

PATHOS

However, Washington's critics were deficient in charity. They failed to realize — or at any rate hated to allow — that the trend was to be anticipated and on the whole to be encouraged. America needed a Saint George; every symbol of national unity was valuable, and Washington was not a mere Federalist puppet. He did genuinely embody aspirations common to nearly all Americans. Even if he had been a weakling, a fool or a bore, which he was not, Washington's popularity would have been a factor of enormous weight. In muttering about it, radically minded Americans were complaining not at an evil but at a blessing that might become too much of a good thing. They were, in true American fashion, unfairly, cruelly and healthily irreverent.

In a deeper sense, Washington's contemporaries ignored the pathos which (perhaps especially to Europeans) is so conspicuous a feature of his achievement, and of American history in general.

Consider, for example, the wistful aspects of Washington's personal situation. He derived satisfaction from doing his duty, and from being so widely admired for it. But unlike some men, he had no relish for public life. The classical code did not lay stress upon pleasure. In enabling other men to pursue happiness according to individual bent, Washington saw his own private existence turn into a hollow shell. The Father of the Nation was himself childless; and however fitting this may be as an item in his historical legend, to the real man it must have been a lasting disappointment to leave no direct heirs. Even his stepson met an early death. As for Mount Vernon, which he had so long labored to improve, Washington was torn away from it for much of his later life. In April 1797, just retired from the Presidency, he found so many repairs necessary that he wrote, with a tired jocularity:

> I am already surrounded by Joiners, Masons, Painters, &c; and such is my anxiety to get out of their hands, that I have scarcely a room to put a friend into, or to sit in myself without the music of hammers, or the odoriferous smell of paint.

And the brief peace he gained there at the end was disturbed by threats of war.

There is, of course, an element of pathos in every human scheme. At the last count, as Marcus Aurelius testifies, nothing matters but mortality:

Call to mind, say the times of Vespasian. It is the same old spectacle – marriage, and child-bearing, disease and death, war and revelry, commerce and agriculture, toadyism and obstinacy; one man praying that heaven may be pleased to take so-and-so, another grumbling at his lot, another in love or laying up treasure, others, again, lusting after consulships and kingdoms. All these have lived their life and their place knows them no more. So pass on to the reign of Trajan. All again is the same, and that life, too, is no more.

But there is a particular pathos to Washington's career, in the disparity between its public and its private sides. What he touched on behalf of the state appeared to succeed triumphantly; what he did for himself seems oddly ephemeral. His very birthplace, in Westmoreland County, Virginia, vanished in flames in 1779. Mount Vernon, though a cherished estate, was an unprofitable one, for the plight of the tidewater planters was not solved by the revolution or by any subsequent event. It was inherent in the poor soil and torrid weather that all Washington's care and thought were unable to vanquish. Drought, insects and disease were more implacable than human enemies.

The leaves of the locust Trees this year, as the last, began to fade, and many of them to dye. The Black Gum Trees, which I had transplanted to my avenues or Serpentine Walks, and which put out leaf and looked well at first, are all dead; so are the Poplars and most of the Mulberrys. The Crab apple trees also, which were transplanted into the shrubberies, and the Papaws are also dead, as also the Sassafras in a great degree. The Pines wholly, and several of the Cedars, as also the Hemlock almost entirely.

This diary extract of July 1785 records an exceptionally bad summer. Yet it is not an isolated example. In other seasons, holly hedges failed; so did a honey-locust hedge around the vineyard. Some golden pheasants he imported languished and gave up the ghost. He laid out a deer park; the deer continually escaped and gnawed his nearby saplings, until after a few years, the park had to be abandoned. The struggle was unremitting and disheartening, as if the Providence he sometimes invoked did not intend George Washington to fashion a permanent dwelling place. Granted even a capable heir, even with devoted and expensive management Mount Vernon could ultimately be nothing but a ruin set in second-growth wilderness, or else an artificially tended shrine.

America was moving away inland to the west. There too, however, Washington's touch lacked magic. He owned extensive tracts, but had decided several years before his death that western lands were a source of more trouble than income. What of the Potomac Company, which had planned to make the river a navigable route to the trans-Allegheny west? Washington had lavished energy and optimism upon the project; the Virginia legislature believed that the results would be "durable monuments of his glory." Alas, the company was doing badly even before he died, and went bankrupt thirty years later. Though the Chesapeake & Ohio Canal promoters absorbed the old Potomac Company, planning to link Washington, D.C., with Pittsburgh, they never got further than Cumberland, in 1850, at the foot of the Alleghenies. George Washington had first gone there (when it was known as Wills Creek) as far back as 1753, on his earliest errand for Governor Dinwiddie. So much effort, and so little to show for it.

The same could be said of other enterprises in which he embarked; not that they were ill conceived but that they were usually ill fated. Thus, Washington was sincerely and commendably interested in founding a national university, in the District of Columbia, to draw together youths from all parts of the Union. He allotted it fifty Potomac shares in his will; but for various reasons this clause of the will remained inoperative.

As for his association with the Federalists — an association that he finally acknowledged — the party came down in resounding defeat shortly after his death, and never regained presidential office. Indeed, it disintegrated as a political force. His own reputation suffered for a few years through the wreck; the Washington Monument seemed almost to have been overthrown in the opening decade of the new century.

All this, perhaps, his contemporaries were hardly in a position to appreciate, any more than they could assess the limitations of his supposedly large fortune. There is a profounder pathos that also has become more distinct with the passage of time. It lies in the role of the hero leader, particularly the President, in the United States. Whether or not the pattern could have been different — if, for instance, his personality had been less "classical," or if some other man had been the first President — Washington did in fact unwittingly set it, as far as essentials were concerned. By the end of his second administration, the President was defined — loosely, contradictorily, yet permanently — as something between monarch, prime minister, party chief and father figure; as a transcendental yet a representative being, a timeless Delphic oracle whose words will endure forever *and* a fallible creature who is an immediate and tempting target for abuse (we find a poet like Philip Freneau treating Washington in both these ways).

In maintaining so much punctilio, Washington perhaps increased his difficulties. Perhaps by the close of his Presidency he had ceased to be fully representative of America's future, however finely he symbolized her past and present. The nineteenth century would add other kinds of heroes to the roster. One of them, Andrew Jackson, was a raw congressman in 1796, who with eleven others – a small, truculent minority, the cloud shaped like a man's hand, clenched – voiced their disapproval of a warm valedictory address to be made by Congress to the retiring President. The era of the Jacksonian common man would prize somewhat different qualities from those we have ascribed to Washington.

Yet Washington was bound to make some tactical errors and to give offense here and there. No one can be all things to all men, as he was required to be. If he had behaved more like a republican general and less like a so-called Eastern monarch, he would still have been disparaged; indeed, the outcome might have been disastrous for the United States. The role of the President, in short, is a strange, vulgar-lofty conception, at the very core of the American mystery. It demands solemnity and yet invites scurrility. He is almost like one of those primitive kings in Frazer's *Golden Bough* who reign in pomp until they are ritually put to death (except, maybe, that the American ruler undergoes slow torture long *before* his final extinction). The urge to worship and the urge to denigrate seem complementary – a uniquely uncomfortable circumstance for Washington, since he entered office as more of a public hero than any other American statesman has been. During his administration – Washington was no exception – the President is supposed to reveal miraculous wisdom and foresight, and also to be an ordinary man. Modern occupants of the White House, a building Washington never occupied, are in material respects handsomely rewarded. The nation accords them salaries, pensions and perquisites on a "monarchical" or "imperial" scale that would have led Washington's contemporaries to impeach him for comparable excesses, and probably to abolish the Presidency itself. But modern Presidents, despite the power, prestige and affluence that envelops them, have known bitter disappointment. George Washington's sense of frustration may have been greater than theirs. The mood in January 1797, on the brink of Washington's retirement, was such that Jefferson could write to James Madison that the President was "fortunate to get off just as the bubble is bursting, leaving others to hold the bag."

John Adams's petulant comments on Washington are significant here. It was, he maintains, egotistical of Washington to serve without salary, and equally wrong to seek retirement after eight years of military command (Adams wrote before Washington became President).

> In wiser and more virtuous times he would not have [done] that, for that is an ambition. He would still be content to be Governor of Virginia, President of Congress, a member of the Senate, or the House of Representatives.

The proper course, apparently, would have been to carry on in harness like some celestial work horse. The rewards of such virtue are honorific – and largely posthumous.

We are accustomed to think of the American outlook as pragmatic and down-to-earth. So it is, in part; and so, in fact, was Washington's mentality. But in comparison with the dense, worldly British texture from which it derived, it is surprisingly thin, diffuse and romantic (and so was Washington as the impalpable hero of legend). Rear Admiral Horatio Nelson, C.B., rising from his dinner on the eve of the battle of Aboukir Bay, could wipe his mouth and predict, "Before this time tomorrow I shall have gained a peerage or Westminster Abbey." His estimate was exact, being based on the realities of British society. The battle was won, and the victor duly dubbed Baron Nelson of the Nile. More than that, Parliament gave him a pension of two thousand pounds a year, the East India Company a bonus of ten thousand pounds; the King of Naples conferred a dukedom with an annual income valued at three thousand pounds; and in Lady Hamilton he acquired a voluptuous mistress. After he was killed at Trafalgar, it is true that Nelson missed interment at Westminster; however, he was buried instead with equivalent glory in St. Paul's Cathedral.

Contrast the lot of Washington, lonely and harassed in his soldierly endeavors, required to combine caution, audacity and humility in impossible proportions; lonely and harassed through the same causes while Chief Executive, with few precedents to guide him (though exalted, as American leaders often are, by the inordinate severity of the task); a sort of splendid foundling at the head of a foundling nation, who survives the ordeal by meeting it with the maximum of cool dignity and the minimum of ideology or introspection. Nelson's recompense is handsome and actual, Washington's mainly metaphorical. No glittering stars upon his breast – many of his countrymen felt that it would be indiscreet, to say the least, to wear even the order of the Cincinnati. No majesty of address — the one is Viscount Nelson, Duke of Brontë, the other, plain Mr. President. He has a coat of arms painted on his coach, but that would be judged a ridiculous affectation in later Presidents. His head is not to appear on the coinage until he is safely dead. No doubt these were wise prejudices, as Washington well comprehended, for a young republic to express. No doubt it was for the best that executive office should be made as unattractive as possible, men being the greedy, ambitious creatures that they are. But how spare and ungenial it sounds. Or how niggardly; Congress took until 1860 to commission and unveil the equestrian statue voted him in 1783; and the giant monument in Washington, D.C., was not finished and dedicated — the culmination of decades of squabbling — until 1885, nearly fourscore and seven years after the demise of the man it commemorates.[11]

Think of Mount Vernon — sun cracking its tired soil, rain eating gullies in the fields around the mansion, hot wind withering the ornamental foliage, weeds encroaching.[12] Mount Vernon, descending through a nephew, and then a nephew of a nephew, worthy, impoverished men, rescued at last, not by Congress, but by the private efforts of the Mount Vernon Ladies' Association and by the oratorical spate of those who raise funds on its behalf. Does not the sagging drama recall the lines of Emerson's "Hamatreya"?

Here is the land,
Shaggy with wood,
With its old valley,
Mound and flood.
But the heritors? —
Fled like the flood's foam.
The lawyer, and the laws,
And the kingdom,
Clean swept herefrom.

---

[11] His mother's grave at Fredericksburg, where she died in 1789, was unmarked by any memorial until 1833. The fifty-foot obelisk then planned was not completed until 1894!

[12] It was in better shape, we should add, than Jefferson's Monticello as a visitor saw it in 1839, only thirteen years after the owner's death. "Around me I beheld nothing but ruin and change, rotting terraces, broken cabins, the lawn ploughed up and cattle wandering among Italian mouldering vases, and the place seemed the true representation of the fallen fortunes of the great man and his family. . . . It was with difficulty I could restrain my tears, and I could not but exclaim, what is human greatness." (Margaret B. Smith, The First Forty Years of Washington Society, New York, 1906, pp. 382-83).

TRIUMPH

Does it, though? Not really. The kingdom is still there in Washington's case, although it happens to be a republic. So are the heritors, although they are a whole nation.

To end on a flat note would be wrong. As with the careers of most great men, there *is* a deeply sad flavor to the life of Washington. It is poignant to inspire awe rather than intimate affection, to have the warm flesh strike cold like marble, because one's temperament was thus, and because America insisted on such frozen excellence. It is melancholy to be entrusted with vast responsibilities, as aware as Washington was of one's own shortcomings. It is grim to be plunged into an endless sequence of war, controversy and crisis, walking the knife edge of catastrophe.

Yet Washington's is also a deeply satisfying record. Here was a man who did what he was asked to do, and whose very strength resided in a sobriety some took for fatal dullness; who in his own person *proved* the soundness of America. A good man, not a saint; a competent soldier, not a great one; an honest administrator, not a statesman of genius; a prudent conserver, not a brilliant reformer. But in sum an exceptional figure.

His, to reiterate, was the goodness of good sense. He was sensible; or, in the supposed jibe of General Charles Lee, he revealed "that rascally virtue, *prudence.*" Prudence or good sense is not a spectacular quality. Good sense rarely makes for wit. Often it involves keeping quiet while others talk. Yet it is recognizable, and usually recognized. The person with good sense, and a leader's temperament, is appealed to, is appointed to preside, to regulate, to decide. People who lack phlegmatic authority, on the other hand, give themselves away – by being indecisive or conceited or devious, or by trying too hard to impress. Occasionally even Washington made mistakes: for instance, in believing too readily that Edmund Randolph was guilty of conspiring with the French. Oncoming age probably accounted for increasing moments of fuss and irritability in his last years. He was undoubtedly less brilliant than Jefferson or Hamilton. But he was also more straightforward – a point maintained in a famous oration of 1828 by John Randolph of Roanoke (himself, by the way, not noted for prudence). Randolph argued that the qualities needed to head a government, or an army, were quite different from those that distinguished logicians and scholars. Indeed, men of learning were *per se* "unfit to be rulers." "Who believes," asked Randolph, "that Washington could write as good a book or report as Jefferson, or make as able a speech as Hamilton?" Such "learned and accomplished men find their proper place under those" – meaning Washington – "who are fitted to command, and to command them among the rest. Such a man as Washington will say to a Jefferson, do you become my Secretary of State; to Hamilton, do you take charge of my purse, or that of the nation, which is the same thing. . . ."

Randolph ranks Cromwell and Hannibal with Washington among natural leaders. Randolph does not speculate on whether such men actively seek the positions they are fitted for. We have suggested that Washington was exceptionally unassuming in demeanor. This was how he appeared to the aristocratic Brissot de Warville, who visited Mount Vernon in 1788. General Washington, said Warville, revealed a modesty "astonishing to a Frenchman; he speaks of the American war, and of his victories, as of things in which he had no direction." Washington was of course well aware that he *had* played the major part in the War for Independence, and that he was about to be summoned back as civilian leader. The "diffidence" Warville detected was that of a person who had gained the heights. Being human, Washington must have derived a powerful inner satisfaction from his renown. At peace with himself, he could usually display tolerance (for example, of religions other than his own: he attended a Roman Catholic mass during the Philadelphia Convention). He could detachedly realize the moral and economic weaknesses of chattel slavery, and plan the eventual manumission of Mount Vernon's black work force. A cynic might say he could afford to be modest.

His private solace was to know at the last that his path had been straightforward and honorable, that he was dying in the house he liked better than anywhere else on earth, watched over by the wife to whom he had been faithful for forty years. His public achievement is the inverse measure. He died knowing that America was intact, that he as much as any person had assisted in its formation, and that while his own sands ran out, time was still on the side of his country. It was an achievement of far more permanent effect than most in history. One of the greatest ironies is the difference between his historical reputation and that of George III. "Farmer George," actually a frugal, conscientious monarch, with tastes quite similar to those of George Washington, managed to be on the losing side. He lived too long, becoming senile and blind. The American George, by contrast, is one of history's great winners; and he had the luck to die before senility threatened him.

How much of the credit is due to him alone we cannot say; in the final analysis the question in irrelevant. He had become so merged with America that his is one of the names on the land, the presence in the air.

Useless for his biographers to try to separate Washington from the myths and images surrounding him – the visage on the postage stamp and on the dollar bill, so familiar that no one sees it, the horseman on the Confederate seal, Andrew Jackson running for the Presidency (oblivious of his early strictures) as the "second Washington," the cherry tree, Cincinnatus at the plow, the grinding ice in the Delaware, the imaginary Indian chief at the Monongahela who declared that no mortal bullet could dispatch George Washington. None can. The man *is* the monument; the monument *is* America. *Si monumentum requiris, circumspice.*

Acknowledgments

I wish to thank:

THE Oxford University Press for permission to cite the World's Classics translation of *The Meditations of Marcus Aurelius;* the Commonwealth Fund and Ford Foundation for enabling me to visit and revisit the United States; my former wife, Mitzi; the late Wallace E. Davies for a tour of Virginia; Warner Moss for hospitality at Williamsburg; Bill Kohlmann for a ride to Mount Vernon; Dorothy Brothers for retyping a much-revised manuscript, in the ideal surroundings of the Center for Advanced Study in the Behavioral Sciences, Stanford, California; Marc Jaffe for friendly editorial help; Fritz Stern for reading and commenting on portions of the proof; Irving Kristol for printing some of my comments on Washington in *Encounter;* the staffs of various libraries, in particular the New-York Historical Society, the New York Public Library, and Manchester University; and my one-time colleagues Maldwyn Jones and Allen Potter.

More recently, I am indebted to: the perfectly named George Washington University, in Washington, D.C., for appointing me to a professorship; Roger Kennedy, director of the National Museum of American History, and his associate, Margaret Klapthor; Wilcomb E. Washburn of the Smithsonian Institution; Barney Mergen, Robert Walker and other GWU friends; Charles Moser, also of GWU, for a visit to Washington's birthplace; Christine Meadows, curator at Mount Vernon, and her predecessor Cecil Wall, himself the author of a readable biography, *George Washington: Citizen Soldier* (Charlottesville, U of Virginia Press, 1980); Shonda Cortez for research assistance and more typing; and John Updike for permission to quote a stanza from his "February 22" in *Telephone Poles and Other Poems* (New York, Alfred A. Knopf, 1963).

The mistakes in this book are, however, either original with me or else borrowed in good faith from the long line of earnest, honorable and humanly fallible biographies of George Washington.

Further Reading

There have been hundreds of biographies and interpretations of Washington. No doubt there will be hundreds more. He has been presented as a businessman, as a man of letters, as a naval genius. Books have been written on topics as specialized as Washington and Freemasonry, on his associations with the Irish, or on Washington and the town of Reading, Pennsylvania. Marvin Kitman has produced an amusingly irreverent study, *George Washington's Expense Account* (New York, 1970), which seeks to portray George Washington as the father of expense-account wizardry. There is even a charming life of Washington in Latin prose (by an Ohio schoolmaster, Francis Glass, published 1835) in which we are told of the great deeds of those latter-day Romans, Georgius Washingtonius, Thomas Jeffersonius, Thomas Pickneyus and the rest.

Most of this bulk of material is dull and repetitive. Some estimates, though – for example, by Chateaubriand, Guizot, or Henry Tuckerman – have held their value through a century or more. Others, notably the account by Mason Weems, are fascinating in their very unreliability. John Marshall's judicially impersonal biography, originally published in five vols. (1804-07), was reprinted in 1832, slightly shortened and without the largely irrelevant first volume. This edition is being reissued (New York, 1981) with an introduction by Marcus Cunliffe. The same editor has supplied an introduction for Woodrow Wilson's, potboiling though not altogether uninteresting *George Washington* (1896; reprinted New York, 1969). Washington Irving's smoothly written five-volume *Washington,* done mainly in the 1850s, was brought out in an abridged version (Tarrytown, 1975) with an introduction by Richard B. Morris.

The indispensable modern biography is that in six volumes by Douglas Southall Freeman (New York, 1948-54), which had got as far as 1793 when its distinguished author died. A seventh and final volume, by his associates John Alexander Carroll and Mary Wells Ashworth, *George Washington: First in Peace,* appeared in 1957, and deserves to be ranked with the others. Freeman is especially good on George Washington's youthful career (which he assesses at the end of Vol. 2); and there is a careful estimates of George Washington's military talent at the end of Vol. 5. Richard Harwell has compressed the whole of Freeman into a one-volume *Washington* (New York, 1968) that contains about a quarter of the original text, without footnotes. A more recent multi-volume biography, breezily written and especially interesting on George Washington's later life, is James T. Flexner's *George Washington* (Boston, 1965-72), available also in abridged form as *The Indispensable Man* (Boston, 1974). A good monographic treatment is Paul Boller, Jr., *George Washington and Religion* (Dallas, 1963). The best of the "debunking" lives, though it does not go beyond the Revolutionary War, is by Rupert Hughes (3 vols., New York, 1926-30). Among the superior one-volume studies are Shelby Little, *George Washington* (New York, 1929); Francis R. Bellamy, *The Private Life of George Washington* (New York, 1951); and Esmond Wright, *Washington and the American Revolution* (London, 1957). James M. Smith has edited *George Washington: A Profile* (New York, 1969), a good collection of appraisals. Another useful selection, which includes contemporary comment, is Morton Borden, ed., *George Washington (Great Lives Observed;* Englewood Cliffs, N.J., 1969).

Apart from these, the best approach to George Washington is through his own words and those of his contemporaries, His *Diaries* (4 vols., Boston, 1925) were edited by John C. Fitzpatrick, who also edited George Washington's *Writings* (39 vols., Washington, D.C., 1931-44). These are now being superseded by excellent new scholarly editions, such as the Washington *Diaries* edited by Donald Jackson and Dorothy Twohig (6 vols., Charlottesville, 1976-79). There are convenient one-volume selections of George Washington compiled by Saxe Commins (New York, 1948) and by Saul K. Padover (New York, 1955). *George Washington in the Ohio Valley* (Pittsburgh, 1955), edited by Hugh Cleland, brings together George Washington's narrative of the seven journeys he made into to the upper Ohio valley between 1753 and 1794. As for George Washington's contemporaries, the two basic old collections were prepared by Jared Sparks (*Correspondence of the American Revolution, being Letters of Eminent Men to Washington, 1775-1789,* 4 vols., Boston, 1853) and by Stanislaus M. Hamilton (*Letters of Washington and Accompanying Papers,* 5 vols., Boston, 1898-1902).

CHAPTER ONE: THE WASHINGTON MONUMENT

For this, see Dixon Wecter, *The Hero in America* (New York, 1941); Marshall Fishwick, *American Heroes: Myth and Reality* (Washington, 1954); William A. Bryan, *George Washington in American Literature, 1775-1865* (New York, 1952), a particularly useful guide; W. S. Baker, ed., *Character Portraits of Washington* (Philadelphia, 1887); Gilbert Chinard, ed., *George Washington as the French Knew Him* (Princeton,

1940); and Frances D. Whittemore, *George Washington in Sculpture* (Boston, 1933).

A good deal of recent scholarship has focused on the heroic and mythological aspects of George Washington. See, for instance, Bernard Mayo, *Myths and Men: Patrick Henry, George Washington, Thomas Jefferson* (Athens, GA., 1959); "The Mythologizing of George Washington," in Daniel J. Boorstin, *The Americans: The National Experience* (New York, 1965); Robert P. Hay, "George Washington: American Moses," in *American Quarterly* 21 (Winter 1969); Lawrence J. Friedman, "The Flawless America," in his *Inventors of the Promised Land* (New York, 1975); Elinor Horwitz, "George Washington," in *The Bird, The Banner and Uncle Sam* (Philadelphia, 1976); and the rich variety of references in Michael Kammen, *A Season of Youth: The American Revolution and the Historical Imagination* (New York, 1978). Southern parallels are brought out in Thomas L. Connelly, *The Marble Man: Robert E. Lee and His Image in American Society* (New York, 1977). George Washington's importance as exemplary hero is stressed in Seymour Martin Lipset, *The First New Nation: The United States in Historical and Comparative Perspective* (New York, 1963). Bruce Mazlish, however, discussing "The Psychological Dimension" in *Leadership and the American Revolution* (Library of Congress symposium, Washington, D.C., 1974), argues that Washington and his associates were not "charismatic" in the proper sense of the word: they did not live ascetically, or claim to embody the soul of their people.

Gerald W. Johnson, *Mount Vernon: the Story of a Shrine* (New York, 1953), is an attractive "account of the rescue and rehabilitation of Washington's home by the Mount Vernon Ladies' Association." *The Washingtoniana* (Baltimore, 1800, and in various subsequent editions) gives a striking view of George Washington's contemporary reputation. George Washington's most popular biographer is described in Harold Kellock, *Parson Weems of the Cherry-Tree* (New York, 1928). Marcus Cunliffe has edited *Weems' Life of Washington* (Cambridge, Mass., 1962) for the John Harvard Library. Latin-American sentiment is expressed in such publications as *Homenaje de la Sociedad bolivariana del Ecuador a Jorge Wáshington, 4 de julio de 1932* (Quito, 1932). George Washington's renown, as early as the 1780s and in places as separated as Cuba and Russia, is documented in *The Impact of the American Revolution Abroad* (Washington, D.C., 1976), a Library of Congress symposium.

CHAPTER TWO: GEORGE WASHINGTON, ESQUIRE

There is a helpful guide through genealogical mazes in an appendix,

"The Washington Family," to Vol. 14 of Worthington C. Ford's edition of *The Writings of George Washington* (New York, 1893), pp. 317-431. A delightful essay on "The Young Washington," by Samuel Eliot Morison, is reprinted in his *By Land and by Sea: Essays and Addresses* (New York, 1953). This essay comments on George Washington's fondness for Addison's play *Cato*. Further light on this aspect of George Washington's tastes is shed by Paul L. Ford, *Washington and the Theatre* (New York, 1889). Paul Van Dyke, *George Washington: The Son of His Country, 1732-1775* (New York, 1931) is an agreeable and accurate study, superseded however by Bernhard Knollenberg's more astringent *George Washington: The Virginia Period* (Durham, N.C., 1964). Lee McCardell, *Ill-Starred General: Braddock of the Coldstream Guards* (Pittsburgh, 1958) stoutly defends this British soldier, and puts into perspective George Washington's own part in the campaign of 1755.

On George Washington's Virginia background, see Thomas P. Abernethy, *Western Lands and the American Revolution* (New York, 1937); Charles H. Ambler, *George Washington and the West* (Chapel Hill, N.C., 1936); and Louis K. Koontz, *The Virginia Frontier, 1754-1763* (Baltimore, 1925), for analyses of trans-Allegheny problems. The Southern mind has been compendiously examined by Richard Bealle Davis, most notably in *Intellectual Life in the Colonial South, 1588-1763* (3 vols., Knoxville, Tenn., 1978) and *A Colonial Southern Bookshelf: Reading in the Eighteenth Century* (Athens, Ga., 1979). For conditions nearer home, see Carl Bridenbaugh, *Myths and Realities: Societies of the Colonial South* (Baton Route, 1952) and *Seat of Empire: The Political Role of Eighteenth-Century Williamsburg* (Williamsburg, 1950), and Charles S. Sydnor, *Gentlemen Freeholders: Political Practices in Washington's Virginia* (Chapel Hill, N.C., 1952).

The gathering crisis of 1763-1775 has been examined by scores of writers. J.C. Miller, *Origins of the American Revolution* (Boston, 1943), and Lawrence H. Gipson, *The Coming of the Revolution* (New York, 1954), are sensible lacunas. On military aspects see John W. Shy, *Toward Lexington: The Role of the British Army in the Coming of the American Revolution* (Princeton, N.J., 1965) and Robert A. Gross, *The Minutemen and Their World* (New York, 1976); Bernard Bailyn, *Ideological Origins of the American Revolution* (Cambridge, Mass., 1967); Edwin G. Burrows and Michael Wallace, "The American Revolution: The Ideology and Psychology of National Liberation," *Perspectives in American History* 6 (1972); Pauline Maier, *From Resistance to Revolution: Colonial Radicals and the Development of American Opposition to Britain, 1765-1776* (New York, 1972); *The Development of a Revolutionary Mentality* (Library of Congress symposium, Washington, D.C., 1972); and parts of Stephen G. Kurtz and James H. Hutson, eds., *Essays on the American Revolution* (Chapel Hill, N.C., 1973). The perplexities of George III and his ministers are discussed in Bernard Donoughue, *British Politics and the American Revolution 1773-1775* (London, 1964). George Washington's own contribution is examined in Curtis P. Nettels, *George Washington and American Independence* (Boston, 1951).

CHAPTER THREE: GENERAL WASHINGTON

John R. Alden, *The American Revolution, 1775-1783* (New York, 1954), is a competent guide. Also to be recommended is John C. Miller, *Triumph of Freedom* (Boston, 1948). The general military situation is recounted in Willard M. Wallace, *Appeal to Arms: A Military History of the American Revolution* New York, 1951), in some of the chapters of Eric Robson, *The American Revolution in its Political and Military Aspects* (London, 1955), with scholarly breadth by Don Higginbotham, *The War of American Independence* (New York, 1971), and with sparkling originality in Charles Royster, *A Revolutionary People at War: The Continental Army and American Character, 1775-1783* (Chapel Hill, 1980). There are some acute essays, for instance on the importance of the militia, in John Shy, *A People Numerous and Armed* (New York, 1976). George A. Billias, ed., *George Washington's Generals* (New York, 1964), contains biographical assessments. For contemporary comments, see the compilation by Frank Moore, *Diary of the American Revolution from Newspapers and Original Documents* (2 vols., New York, 1860); Herbert T. Wade and Robert A. Lively, eds., *This Glorious Cause: The Adventures of Two Company Officers in Washington's Army* (Princeton, 1958); and George F. Scheer and Hugh F. Rankin, *Rebels and Redcoats* (New York, 1957) – a useful collection of contemporary eyewitness accounts. To these add John C. Dann, ed., *The Revolution Remembered* (Chicago, 1980).

E. C. Burnett's edition of *Letters of Members of the Continental Congress* (8 vols., Washington, 1921-38), valuable in its day, will eventually be superseded by a more rigorously scholarly collection. The same author has provided a sensible, though dull, commentary in *The Continental Congress* (New York, 1941).

Among the better studies of George Washington's military career are Thomas G. Frothingham, *Washington, Commander in Chief* (Boston, 1930), and – uneven but original, with particular reference to the so-called Conway "Cabal" – Bernhard Knollenberg, *Washington and the Revolution: A Reappraisal* (New York, 1941), together with Theodore

Thayer, *Washington and Lee at Monmouth: The Making of a Scapegoat* (Port Washington, N.Y., 1976). Sympathetic biographies of figures associated with the "Cabal" include John R. Alden, *General Charles Lee* (Baton Rouge, 1951), Samuel W. Patterson, *Horatio Gates* (New York, 1941), and Paul D. Nelson, *General Horatio Gates: A Biography* (Baton Rouge, 1976). Among other biographies of Washington's generals are Martin H. Bush, *Revolutionary Enigma: A Re-Appraisal of General Philip Schuyler of New York* (Port Washington, N.Y., 1969), and Charles Royster's sophisticated study of wartime glamor and postwar let-down, *Light-Horse Harry Lee and the Legacy of the American Revolution* (New York, 1981). Medical aspects are touched upon in Morris H. Saffron, *Surgeon to Washington: Dr. John Cochran, 1730-1807* (New York, 1977), which combines a compact biography with an edition of Cochran's correspondence. There is an abundance of material in the various volumes on Lafayette by Louis Gottschalk (Chicago, 1935-50).

For the British side, see the long apologia by Sir Henry Clinton, *The American Rebellion* (ed. By William B. Willcox, New Haven, 1954); *Journal of Nicholas Cresswell, 1774-1777* (London, 1925); *The American Journal of Ambrose Serle . . . 1776-1778* (ed. By Edward H. Tatum, Jr., San Marino, 1940); Marion Balderston and David Syrett, eds., *The Lost War: Letters from British Officers during the American Revolution* (New York, 1975); and Paul H. Smith, *Loyalists and Redcoats: A Study in British Revolutionary Policy* (Chapel Hill, N.C., 1964). The best account of the war as perceived from London is Piers Mackesy, *The War for America, 1775-1783* (Cambridge, Mass., 1964); and see George A. Billias, ed., *George Washington's Opponents: British Generals and Admirals in the American Revolution* (New York, 1969). Other good biographical studies include William B. Willcox, *Portrait of a General: Sir Henry Clinton in the War of Independence* (New York, 1964); Ira D. Gruber, *The Howe Brothers and the American Revolution* (Chapel Hill, N.C., 1972); and Franklin and Mary Wickwire, *Cornwallis: The American Adventure* (Boston, 1970). For an authoritative reinterpretation of British strategy in Burgoyne's Saratoga campaign, see Gerald S. Brown, *The American Secretary: The Colonial Policy of Lord George Germain, 1775-1778* (Ann Arbor, Mich., 1963). The confidential letters and journals of a Hessian officer, Major Baurmeister, 1776-1784, have been translated and edited by Bernhad A. Uhlendorf, *Revolution in America* (New Brunswick, 1957). One of the most touching Loyalist stories is that of Samuel Curwen, *Journal and Letters* (Boston, 1842). Excellent work has been done on the Loyalists by William H. Nelson, Mary Beth Norton, R. M. Calhoon and other scholars. Gordon S. Wood, *The Creation of the American Republic, 1776-*

1787 (Chapel Hill, N.C., 1969) is a brilliant history of ideas, especially that of republicanism.

William S. Baker, *Washington after the Revolution, 1784-1799* (Philadelphia, 1898), spans the period covered by this chapter. The first part is dealt with in Merrill Jensen, *The New Nation: A History of the United States during the Confederation, 1781-1789* (New York, 1950), and in E. James Ferguson, *The Power of the Purse: A History of American Public Finance, 1776-1790* (Chapel Hill, N.C., 1961), and – among various studies by Jackson T. Main – his *Political Parties Before the Constitution* (Chapel Hill, N.C., 1973). For the troubles in Massachusetts associated with Daniel Shays, see Marion L. Starkey, *A Little Rebellion* (New York, 1955); Joseph P. Warren, "The Confederation and the Shays Rebellion," *American Historical Review* 11 (1905); J. R. Pole, *Political Representation in England and the Origins of the American Republic* (London, 1966), 226-44; and Van Beck Hall, *Politics Without Parties: Massachusetts, 1780-1791* (Pittsburgh, 1972). The Constitutional Convention has been described by Max Farrand, Carl Van Doren, Charles Warren and others; and see especially Max Farrand, ed., *Records of the Federal Convention of 1787* (4 vols., New Haven, 1911-37). There are several resourceful studies of the politics, economics and ideology of the era: Richard Buel, Jr., *Securing the Revolution: Ideology in American Politics, 1789-1815* (Ithaca, N.Y., 1972); E. A. J. Johnson, *The Foundations of American Freedom: Government and Enterprise in the Age of Washington* (Minneapolis, 1973); Curtis P. Nettels, *The Emergence of a National Economy, 1775-1815* (New York, 1962); John Zvesper, *Political Philosophy and Rhetoric: A Study of the Origins of American Party Politics* (Cambridge, 1977); Lance Banning, *The Jeffersonian Persuasion: Evolution of a Party Ideology* (Ithaca, N.Y., 1978); and Drew R. McCoy, *The Elusive Republic: Political Economy in Jeffersonian America* (Chapel Hill, N.C., 1980).

On George Washington's Presidency, a full and readable account is Nathan Schachner, *The Founding Fathers* (New York, 1954). The first steps are investigated in James Hart, *The American Presidency in Action, 1789* (New York, 1948). Leonard D. White, *The Federalists* (New York, 1948), is an excellent administrative study; and see the same author's "George Washington as an Administrator" (1944), reprinted in Edward N. Saveth, ed., *Understanding the American Past* (Boston, 1954), pp. 144-57. On George Washington's passive role as "candidate" see essay by Marcus Cunliffe in *History of American Presidential Elections,*

4 vols., ed. By Arthur M. Schlesinger, Jr., and Fred L. Israel (New York, 1971), vol. I. Early American military policy is eruditely discussed in Richard H. Kohn, *Eagle and Sword: The Federalists and the Creation of the Military Establishment in America, 1783-1802* (New York, 1975). An old work that still has some value is *The Republican Court, or American Society in the Days of Washington* (New York, 1854), by Rufus W. Griswold (who wrote much more sympathetically on George Washington than he did on Edgar Allan Poe, for whom he served as literary executioner rather than literary executor).

With the *Journal of William Maclay,* edited by Edgar S. Maclay (New York, 1890), we plunge into controversy. We remain there, on the same side of the argument, with Charles Warren, *Jacobin and Junto: or, Early American Politics as Viewed in the Diary of Dr. Nathaniel Ames, 1758-1822* (Cambridge, Mass., 1931). The unpopularity of George Washington among Republican journalists is made clear by James D. Tagg, "Benjamin Franklin Bache's Attack on George Washington," *Pennsylvania Magazine of History and Biography* 100 (April 1976). See also John R. Howe, "Republican Thought and the Political Violence of the 1790s," *American Quarterly* 19 (1967), and Marshall Smelser, "The Federalist Period as an Age of Passion," *American Quarterly* 10 (1958). There are detailed biographies of Thomas Jefferson (by Dumas Malone and by Merrill Peterson) and of James Madison (notably by Irving Brant). Leland D. Baldwin, *Whiskey Rebels* (Pittsburgh, 1939), deals with the unrest in Pennsylvania, and see Jacob E. Cooke, "The Whiskey Insurrection: A Re-Evaluation," *Pennsylvania History* 30 (1963). Noble E. Cunningham, Jr., *The Jeffersonian Republicans* (Chapel Hill, N.C., 1958) is a close study of party organization from 1789 to 1801. The same period is discussed with intelligent asperity in Joseph Charles's *Origins of the American Party System* (Williamsburg, 1956). On the Federalist side, there is a contemporary defense in George Gibbs, ed., *Memoirs of the Administrations of Washington and Adams from the Papers of Oliver Wolcott* (2 vols., New York, 1846). John C. Miller's *Alexander Hamilton: Portrait in Paradox* (New York, 1959) is fair-minded and scholarly. Early argument over what to call President Washington is amusingly sketched by James H. Hutson, "John Adams' Title Campaign," *New England Quarterly* 41 (March 1968). The career of Adams has been well discussed in biographical works by Page Smith, John R. Howe and Peter Shaw. Stephen G. Kurtz is excellent on *The Presidency of John Adams* (Philadelphia, 1957). The old standard work on *Jay's Treaty* by Samuel F. Bemis (New York, 1923) should be supplemented by Jerold A. Combs, *The Jay Treaty: Political Background of the Founding Fathers* (Berkeley, Cal. 1970). George Washington is admirably "placed" in Felix Gilbert, *To the Farewell Address: Ideas of Early American Foreign Policy* (Princeton, N.J., 1961), in Charles R. Ritcheson, *Aftermath of Revolution: British Policy Toward the United States, 1783-1795* (Dallas, 1969), and in Bradford Perkins, *The First Rapprochement: England and the United States, 1795-1805* (Berkeley, Cal., 1967). Alexander DeConde, *Entangling Alliance: Politics and Diplomacy under George Washington* (Durham, N.C., 1958) portrays George Washington as slow-witted and strongly influenced by Hamilton. Forrest McDonald's expert if idiosyncratic *The Presidency of George Washington* (Lawrence, Kansas, 1974) concludes that George Washington was indispensable, "but only for what he was, not for what he did." According to McDonald, George Washington "had done little in his own right, had often opposed the best measures of his subordinates, and had taken credit for achievements that he had no share in bringing about."

Finally, the reader should if possible refer to the collected writings of John Adams, Jefferson, Madison, Monroe, Hamilton and other principal figures of the era. Nearly all wrote remarkably well; and often passion lent them an added eloquence.

CHAPTER FIVE: THE WHOLE MAN

Broadly interpretive essays include: Harold W. Bradley, "The Political Thinking of George Washington" (*Journal of Southern History* 11, 1945, pp. 469-86), Saul K. Padover, "George Washington – Portrait of a True Conservative" (*Social Research* 22, 1955, pp. 199-222), and Edmund S. Morgan, *The Genius of George Washington* (New York, 1980). A perceptive earlier interpretation is in Henry T. Tuckerman, *Essays, Biographical and Critical* (Boston, 1857): "If we may borrow a metaphor from natural philosophy, it was not by magnetism, so much as by gravitation, that [GW's] moral authority was established." François Guizot's intelligent short book, *Essay on the Character and Influence of Washington* (Boston, 1851), was originally an introduction to a French edition of Jared Sparks on George Washington. Various views of George Washington, from the myth "compounded of Stuart's portrait and Greenough's statue of Olympian Jove with Washington's features" to the caricature of him as a loutish squire, "very awkward, very illiterate, and very dull," and including a serious assessment of him as the embodiment of Roman virtue, are set forth in Henry Adams's caustic novel *Democracy* (New York, 1880). The excuse for the symposium on George Washington in Adams's novel is a visit paid by some of the characters to

Mount Vernon. The classical aspects of the epoch are explored in Richard M. Gummere, *The American Colonial Mind and the Classical Tradition* (Cambridge, Mass., 1963). Gummere notes for example that, back in 1756, Colonel Washington's countersign for the sentries at Fort Cumberland was "Xanthippe" (the wife of Socrates). This may have been a joke, since Xanthippe was described as a nagging shrew of a woman. Meyer Reinhold's *The Classick Pages* (University Park, Pa., 1975) is an anthology of classical allusions, in the translations and histories familiar to George Washington's contemporaries. Wilson O. Clough's *Intellectual Origins of American National Thought* (New York, 1961) is another selection that includes examples of the work of favorite classical authors. There is a chapter on classical tastes in Howard Mumford Jones, *O Strange New World, American Culture: The Formative Years* (New York, 1964).

On ideas of aristocracy and monarchy in George Washington's America, see William S. Thomas, *The Society of the Cincinnati, 1783-1935* (New York, 1935); Wallace E. Davies, *Patriotism on Parade: The Story of Veterans' and Hereditary Organizations in America, 1783-1900* (Cambridge, Mass., 1955); and Louise B. Dunbar, *A Study of Monarchical Tendencies in the United States from 1776-1801* (Urbana, 1923). Much recent scholarship has focussed on the argument that republicanism, though a wide-ranging ideology, was of great importance to Washington's America. In part, of course, its emphasis was negative in expressing hostility to monarchy. But this seemingly negative attitude may well have taken a positive form, with Washington and others: see Charles C. Thach, Jr., *The Creation of the Presidency, 1775-1789* (Baltimore, 1922; repr., 1969). Other ramifications (or roads not taken?) are explored in Mary Beth Norton, *Liberty's Daughters: The Revolutionary Experience of American Women, 1750-1800* (Boston, 1980) and Linda K. Kerber, *Women of the Republic: Intellect and Ideology in Revolutionary America* (Chapel Hill, N.C., 1980).

Chronology

1732

22 February George Washington born at family home on Popes Creek (Wakefield), Westmoreland, VA (11 February 1731/32, Old-Style Calendar)

1743

12 April Death of father, Augustine Washington

1749

20 July Appointed surveyor of Culpeper County, Virginia

1751

September–
March 1752 Visited Barbados with half-brother, Lawrence Washington

1752

26 July Death of half-brother, Lawrence Washington

6 November Appointed major in the Virginia militia

1753

31 October Sent by Governor Dinwiddie to deliver ultimatum to the French at Fort Le Boeuf

1754

20 March Assumed command of forces sent on mission to Fort Duquesne

4 July Surrendered to French at Fort Necessity

1755

10 May Appointed volunteer aide-de-camp to General Edward Braddock

9 July Braddock's army defeated, the General is killed; Washington praised for his courage

14 August Appointed Colonel and Commander of Virginia Regiment

1758

24 July Elected Burgess for Frederick County, Virginia

23 November Fort Duquesne abandoned by French; Washington resigned commission

1759

6 January Married Martha Dandridge Custis

1761

18 May Re-elected to House of Burgesses

1762

25 October Appointed vestryman of Truro Parish, Fairfax County

1763
3 October   Appointed warden of Pohick Church, Fairfax County
1765
16 July   Elected to the Virginia House of Burgesses for Fairfax County (re-elected 1768, 1769, 1771, 1774)
1770
October   Justice of the Peace, Fairfax County
1773
May-June   Journey to New York City
1774
July   Member and chairman of meeting that adopted Fairfax County Resolves

August   Attended first Virginia Provincial Convention in Williamsburg

1 August   Elected to attend First Continental Congress in Philadelphia

September-
October   First Continental Congress meets in Philadelphia
1775
May-June   Delegate at Second Continental Congress

16 June   Elected General and Commander in Chief of the Army of the United States

3 July   Took command of Continental troops at Cambridge, Massachusetts
1776
16 March   Washington's troops occupied Boston

27-29 August Battle of Long Island; Americans retreat to Manhattan

28 October   Battle of White Plains, New York

25-26 Dec.   Defeat of Hessians at Trenton, New Jersey
1777
3 January   British defeated at Battle of Trenton; establishment of winter quarters at Morristown, New Jersey

11 September Americans defeated at Battle of Brandywine

4 October   Americans defeated at Battle of Germantown

17 October   Surrender of Burgoyne at Saratoga, New York

Winter   Winter quarters at Valley Forge
1778
18 June   British evacuation of Philadephia

28 June   British defeated at Battle of Monmouth

Winter   Winter quarters at Middlebrook, New Jersey

                                 1780
11 July   Arrival of French fleet and army under command of
               Rochambeau at Newport, Rhode Island
                                 1781
19 October   British under command of Cornwallis surrender at
               Battle of Yorktown, Virginia
                                 1783
15 March   Newburgh Address
8 June   Circular letter to the states
19 June   Elected president-general of the Society of the
               Cincinnati
4 December   Farewell to officers at Fraunces' Tavern, New York City
23 December   Resigned commission to Congress in Annapolis,
               Maryland
                                 1784
December   Attended Annapolis conference on Potomac River
               navigation
                                 1785
25-28 March   Hosted Mount Vernon Conference
17 May   President of the Potomac Company
                                 1787
28 March   Elected Virginia delegate to federal conventio in
               Philadelphia
25 May   Elected president of the convention
17 September   Draft of Constitution signed; convention adjourned
                                 1788
18 January   Elected chancellor of William and Mary College
                                 1789
4 February   Unanimoulsy elected President of the United States
30 April   Inaugurated President at Federal Hall, New York City
25 August   Death of mother, Mary Ball Washington, at
               Fredericksburg, Virginia
October-   Presidential tour of New England (except Rhode Island)
November
                                 1790
August   Visit to Rhode Island
September   Arrived in Philadelphia, new temporary capital of the
               United States
                                 1791
April-June   Presidential tour of the southern United States

1792

5 December	Unanimously re-elected President of the United States

1793

4 March	Inaugurated President for second term at Pennsylvania State House (Independence Hall), Philadelphia
22 April	Issued Proclamation of Neutrality
18 September	Set cornerstone of Capitol in Federal City (Washington, D.C.)
31 December	Resignation of Thomas Jefferson as Secretary of State

1794

November	Declared suppression of "Whiskey Rebellion"

1795

31 Jaunary	Resignation of Alexander Hamilton as Secretary of the Treasury

1796

19 September	Farewell Address (dated 17 September) published in Philadelphia *Daily American Advertiser*

1797

March	Retirement and return to Mount Vernon, following inauguration of John Adams as President

1798

4 July	Appointed Lieutenant General and Commander in Chief of the Armies of the United States

1799

14 December	Death of George Washington at Mount Vernon

1802

22 May	Death of Martha Washington at Mount Vernon

Index

Fort Ticonderoga, New York, 51, 58, 66, 73

Fort Venango, Pennsylvania, 31

Fort Washington, New York, 62, 64

France, wars with Britain, 30, 35, 39, 46, 59, 74, 77; aid to colonies, 71, 74, 78; recognizes United States as nation, 74; alliance, 77, menace, 115-117; naval war, 121. *See also* French troops.

Franklin, Benjamin (1706-1790), 11, 97, 100, 104, 128; in Paris, 74, 83

Fraunces' Tavern, New York, 83, 120

Fredericksburg, Virginia, 29, 30, 46, 210n.

Freemasonry, 14, 30

French fleet, 76-78, 81

French Revolution, 113-114

French troops, in West, 24; stubbornness, 31; Trent ousted by, 32; Duquesne, 33-35, 36, 50; GW eager to oust, 37; ultimatum to, 38; removal of threat, 46; war continued, 50. *See also* France.

Freneau, Philip (1752-1832), 110-111, 119, 122, 142

Gage, General Thomas (1721-1787), 74; Breed's Hill (Bunker Hill), 56-57, 66-67; Duquesne, 56

"Gallomania," "Gallomen," 113, 116, 119

Gates, Horatio (1728-1806), 53, 62, 80; adjutant general, 55; northern army, 74; Conway Cabal, 75-76, 137

Gazette of the United States, 110

Genêt, Citizen (1763-1834), 114-116

George II, 13n., 33

George III, statue replaced by GW's, 8; subjects 48, 133; loyalty to, 56; independence from, 58; "Royal Brute," 58; villain, 59; opposition to, 65; not a monster, 66; connection not severed, 114

Georgia, 66, 46, 80

Germain, Lord George, 58, 66, 69-70

German troops, *See also* Hessians.

Germantown, Pennsylvania, 72, 76

Gist, Christopher, 31-33, 41

Gladstone, William E., 16

Gordon, General, 125

Grasse, Admiral de, 80-81

Great Lakes, 31, 67, 83, 92

Great Meadows, Pennsylvania, 32-33

Greene, General Nathanael, (1742-1786), 64, 72, 79-80, 87

Guilford Court House, North Carolina, 80

Hale, Nathan, 130

Halifax, Nova Scotia, 59-60

Hamilton, Alexander (1755?-1804), 107-108, 117-118, 121, 124, 128, 135; warns of Conway Cabal, 75; urges ratification in New York, 99; Secretary of Treasury, 104; GW relies on, 106; feud with Jefferson, 108-113; revenue system, 114, 116; resigns, 117; death, 121; Act for Establishing a Mint, 138

Hampton, Virginia, 24

Hancock, John (1732?)1793), 59, 99

Hanover County, Virginia, 51

Harlem Heights, New York, 62

Head of Elk, Maryland, 71

Henry, Patrick (1736-1799), 48-49, 51, 55, 79, 128; delegate, 51; disgruntled, 99

Hessians, 59, 63, 82, 97

Holland, 77, 118

Houdon (French sculptor), 9, 91

House of Representatives, 109, 120; authorize monument, 2; formation, 98

Howe, Admiral Lord (1736-1799), 60, 62, 66, 71

Howe, General William (1729-1814), 62-63, 66-69, 73-75, 81; commander in chief, 58; Boston, 58, 60; Staten Island, 60; Long Island, 61, 66; Brooklyn Heights, 61; New York, 62; New Brunswick, 63; knighted, 63; peace commissioner, 66; Newport, 67; opposes Clinton, 68; Philadelphia, 69-72, 74; Brandywine, 71; Germantown, 72, 77, resigns 73

Hudson River, New York, 73, 80, 95

"Humble Address," 36

Humphreys, David, 103

Hunting Creek property, Virginia, 22, 26

Independence, American, 58, 82

Indians, 25, 31-33, 37, 46, 111,115,147; bounty for scalps, 25; treaties with, 28, 118; Wills Creek, 32; Duquesne, 34-35; Boston Tea Party, 49

Jackson, Andrew (1767-1845), 142, 147

Jackson, William, 103

James River, 93

James River Company, 93

Jamestown, Virginia, 20

Jay, John (1745-1829), 75; commissioner to Paris, 82; letters from GW, 94, 96; Foreign Secretary, 94; move for new government, 95; advice to GW, 95-96; Chief Justice, 103; GW consults, 106; Federalist, 112; treaty with England, 115-118, 132

Jefferson, Thomas (1743-1826), 48, 90, 114, 115-119, 128; education compared to GW's 23-24; too ill to be nominated, 50; author of Declaration of Independence, 60, 134; governor of Virginia, 80; nearly captured, 80; recommends Potomac Plan, 95; American minister to Paris, 96; appointed to Department of State, 104; feud with Hamilton, 108-113; Monticello, 111, 211n. resigned, 117; inaugurated President, 121

Jones, John Paul (1747-1792), 79

Judiciary Act, 103

Jumonville, M. de, 32-34, 63

Kalb, Baron De (1721-1780), 74, 80

Kanawha valley, 48, 90

Kentucky, joins Union, 118

Kingston (formerly Esopus), New York, 74

Knox, General Henry (1750-1806), Boston, 58; letter from GW, 100; Secretary of War, 103; with Hamilton, 110

Kosciusko, Thaddeus (1746-1817), 13, 74

Lafayette, Marquis de (1757-1834), 13, 80; mason, 14; key to Bastille, 14; value to American cause, 74; Conway Cabal, 75; leads American forces in Virginia, 80; Yorktown, 81; invites GW to France, 89; GW's bosom friend, 96, 127; urges GW to accept Presidency, 100; leader in France, 114; free again, 120

Lake Erie, 31-32, 51

Laurel Mountain, Pennsylvania, 32

Laurens, Henry (1724-1792), 82

Laurens, John (1754-1782), 127

League of Armed Neutrality, 77

Lear, Tobias, 103

Lee, Charles (1731-1782), military experience; New York, 89; taken prisoner, 90, 99, 115; released, 111; conduct at Monmouth, 111, 186, 189; courtmartial, 111; relegated to insignificance, 117, 128

Lee, Henry (1756-1818), 7, 8, 95

Lee, Richard Henry (1732-1794), 99

Lee, Robert E., 9, 13, 83

Leeward Islands, 39

Lewis, Eleanor Custis, 121

Lexington, Massachusetts, 51

Lincoln, Abraham, 9

Little Hunting Creek tract, 21, 22, 26

London, England, 31, 33, 42, 48, 66, 74, 98, 115

London Magazine, 33

Long Island, New York, 61, 65-66, 71

Loudoun, Lord, 39

Louisburg, Nova Scotia, 48

Louisiana Purchase, 121

McClellan, General George B., 83-84

Mackay, Captain, 38

Maclay, William (1734-1804), 102, 104-105

Madison, James (1751-1836), education compared to GW's 31, 32; Annapolis and Philadelphia conventions, 137; leader for new government, 140, in House of Representatives, 154; close ties with GW, 157; falling-out with GW, 157

Manhattan, New York, 61-62

Marye, Reverend James, 23

Maryland, 25, 28, 52, 93

Mason, George (1725-1792), 48-50, 99

Masons, *See* Freemasonry.

Wolfe, General James, 41

Publications

George Washington: A Brief Biography by William MacDonald. 46 pages, 12 illustrations. Softbound. $2.00

The George Washington Activity Book for Young People by Mary Ann Deary. Illustrations by Kelly St. Clair. 32 pages. Softbound. $2.50

George Washington: Citizen-Soldier by Charles Cecil Wall. 226 pages, 53 illustrations. Softbound. $7.95

George Washington's Rules of Civility & Decent Behaviour in Company and Conversation. Introduction by Letitia Baldrige. Annotated by Ann M. Rauscher. 64 pages, 14 illustrations. Softbound. $5.95

Greetings from Mount Vernon: Historic Postcards from the Mount Vernon Collection Selected and annotated by Carter King Laughlin and Ann M. Rauscher. 24 postcards, ready to mail. Softbound. $4.95

The Last Will and Testament of George Washington. Introduction by the Honorable Lewis F. Powell, Jr. 80 pages. Softbound. $5.95

Maxims of George Washington. Collected and arranged by John Frederick Schroeder. Introduction by Gerald R. Ford. Chapter introductions by John P. Riley. 224 pages, 31 illustrations. Softbound. $7.95

Mount Vernon: A Handbook. 128 pages, 139 color illustrations. Softbound. $3.35

Mount Vernon Coloring Book. Illustrated by Babs Gaillard. 22 pages. Softbound. $2.50

The Mount Vernon Cookbook. 244 pages, 35 line drawings, 7 color illustrations. Spiral-bound. $14.95

Mount Vernon: The Civil War Years by Dorothy Troth Muir. Previously published as *Presence of a Lady.* Introduction by Ernest B. Furgurson. Forewords by Robert E. Lee IV and Ulysses Grant Dietz. 136 pages, 14 illustrations. Softbound. $7.95

Mount Vernon: The Story of a Shrine by Gerald W. Johnson. Epilogue by Ellen McCallister Clark. 176 pages, 34 illustrations. Softbound. $7.95

Nelly Custis: Child of Mount Vernon by David L. Ribblett. Introduction by Julie Nixon Eisenhower. 124 pages, 16 illustrations. Softbound. $7.95

Nothing More Agreeable: Music in George Washington's Family by Judith S. Britt. 124 pages, 51 illustrations, 10 in color. Softbound. $4.95

Where was George Washington? by Carla Heymsfeld. Illustrated by Jennifer Koury. 36-page children's book with color illustrations. Hardbound (French translation also available). $9.95 Softbound. $5.95

George Washington: Pioneer Farmer Coloring and Game Book. Softbound. Illustrations by Babs Gaillard McNear. 32 pages. $3.50

Mount Vernon Hands-On History (A Discovery of 18th-Century Life at the Home of George Washington). Original illustrations by Suzanne Parrish. Written and compiled by Nancy Hayward. 76 pages. Softbound. $3.50

George Washington: Pioneer Farmer by Alan and Donna Jean Fusonie. 66 pages, 14 illustrations. Softbound. $5.95.

AUDIOVISUALS

The Life of George Washington by Robert B. Gibby. Introduced by Senator Bill Bradley. Thirty-minute, full-color videotape. VHS format. $24.95

Mount Vernon: The Home of George Washington by Robert D. Ellis. Thirty-minute, full-color videotape. VHS format. $24.95

Mount Vernon Slide Presentation 40 color slides and cassette. $14.95

Available by mail from The Museum Shop, Mount Vernon Ladies' Association, Mount Vernon, Virginia 22121. Virginia purchases add 4 1/2 percent sales tax. Postage and handling: $3.00 for single volume, $1.00 for each additional volume. All Prices Are Subject To Change.